THE STUDY OF
COMMUNITY
POWER
A BIBLIOGRAPHIC REVIEW

WILLIS D. HAWLEY & JAMES H. SVARA

Santa Barbara, California
Oxford, England

Library of Congress Catalog Card No. 72-83287
SBN Paperbound Edition 0-87436-089-7
Clothbound Edition 0-87436-088-9

American Bibliographical Center - Clio Press, Inc.
2040 Alameda Padre Serra
Santa Barbara, California

European Bibliographical Center-Clio Press
30 Cornmarket Street
Oxford OX1 3EY, England

CONTENTS

PREFACE

Introduction

Over the last several years the study of community power has been the concern of a great deal of social science research and analysis. Despite this extensive literature, consensus among interested students of the subject has yet to develop a set of concepts, research strategies and analytical structures that might facilitate the formulation of propositions and the accumulation of comparable data and thus significantly advance our understanding of community decision making.

This bibliographic study seeks to encourage the growth of consensus on ways to deal with these barriers to further progress in the study of community power. Of course, this book is not solely for scholars or theory builders. Those interested in urban politics will find many of the most important books and articles on city politics summarized in these pages.

Scope of the Bibliography

The three main sections of the book identify a substantial portion of the literature dealing directly with community power that was *published* (including dissertations) during the 50 years preceding 1971. More than 95 percent of the entries are annotated. In one sense, almost everything that happens in and to urban areas relates to community power and thus, in order to prepare a comprehensive listing of material in this field, it was necessary to set some limits on the scope of the items we would include. For our purposes, we defined the study of community power as that scholarly or systematic description and analysis of the structure or pattern of community-wide decision making that is intended to authoritatively allocate significant privilege or resources among various institutions, groups and/or individuals. This seems to us a relatively conventional interpretation of "community power." Thus, we do not include studies of specific institutions or interests (such as nonpartisan elections, the press, or labor and business groups) unless the research deals with their relative influence in the overall pattern of community decision making.[1] We have also excluded studies of subcommunities, though some studies dealing with leadership structures in subcommunities that are ethnic or racial in character are included because of the substantial interest among urbanists in such groups.[2]

Research published in languages other than English has also been excluded though a number of items concerned with community power in other countries have been listed. Material dealing with special issue areas, such as the substantial literature on urban renewal or school desegregation, that does not deal explicitly with the implications for community-wide decision making in other issue areas is not included.[3] Finally, book chapters dealing with community power which are part of works whose primary focus is national politics are not annotated.[4]

Drawing the boundaries as we do on what material is appropriate to include in this bibliography means some books that seem quite important to the development of a theoretical understanding of community power are not cited here. Among the volumes that make especially significant steps toward the development of a theory of community power and should not go unnoted are: (1) James Coleman's short monograph, *Community Conflict* (New York: The Free Press, 1957); (2) Andrew McFarland's *Power and Leadership in Pluralist Systems* (Stanford: Stanford University Press, 1969); and William Gamson's *Power and Discontent* (Homewood, Ill.: Dorsey Press, 1969).

---

[1] For example, we have not listed such important works as *City Manager Government in the United States*, by Harold Stone, Don K. Price, and Kathryn Stone (Chicago: Public Administration Service, 1946); Eugene C. Lee's *The Politics of Nonpartisanship* (Berkeley: Univ. of California Press, 1960); or Morris Janowitz, *The Community Press in an Urban Setting* (Glencoe, Ill.: The Free Press, 1961).

[2] We have not included ethnographic studies which are not primarily concerned with political communities. Thus, Elliot Liebow's *Tally's Corner* (Boston: Little, Brown, and Co., 1966); and *The Urban Villagers* by Herbert Gans (New York: The Free Press, 1962) are not reviewed below.

[3] In retrospect this exclusion seems the most difficult and we should, at least, acknowledge some of the work which, though concerned with specific issues, speaks to the major questions in the study of community power. We refer the reader to: Robert Crain, *The Politics of School Desegregation* (Chicago: Aldine, 1968); Robert L. Crain, Elihu Katz and Donald B. Rosenthal, *The Politics of Community Conflict: The Fluoridation Decision* (Indianapolis: Bobbs-Merrill, 1969); Peter Rossi and Robert Dentler, *The Politics of Urban Renewal* (Glencoe, Ill.: The Free Press, 1961); and Edward C. Banfield and Martin Meyerson, *Politics, Planning and the Public Interest* (New York: The Free Press, 1958).

[4] See for example, Arnold Rose, *The Power Structure* (New York: Oxford Univ. Press, 1968), Chs. 8-9; and William Domhoff, *Who Rules America?* (Englewood Cliffs, N.J.: Prentice-Hall, 1968), Ch. 6.

The Organization of the Book

Chapter One provides the reader with a brief history of the study of community power from the Lynds' work in Middletown to current efforts to develop a theory of community power based on comparative studies. Major works in the development of this area of research are noted and the changing nature of the issues that dominate the field are discussed. Suggestions for the directions in which future research needs to move are outlined.

The second chapter lists and summarizes reports of field research conducted in one or more communities. In most cases the annotations identify the site of the study, the size and social character of the community, the methodology employed by the author and the major findings and conclusions. We do not (consciously) offer any critical judgement on the material surveyed.

One of the unique contributions of this bibliography is that an effort has been made to include citations to book reviews which have appeared in scholarly journals. While no effort was made to catalog such commentaries published prior to 1960, we have examined the post-1959 reviews in journals serving political scientists and sociologists. Reviews are listed following the citation of the book to which they refer.

In this chapter, and in chapters Three and Four, we have listed doctoral dissertations dealing more or less directly with community power. Most of the items cited have been written since 1965. The identification of many of these dissertations was facilitated by Datrix, a service of University Microfilms Inc. The dissertation citations are not annotated though most may be reviewed by consulting Dissertation Abstracts.

Chapter Three identifies the substantial body of literature which focuses on problems of research and analysis of data from community settings. The annotations are generally shorter than those in the previous chapter and describe the authors' central arguments and conclusions.

Chapter Four is, in a sense, a residual category into which fall secondary analyses of case studies, observations on the implications of community power studies for democratic theory and other material. As in the preceding two sections, most of the items cited are summarized.

The final chapter in the book identifies a large number of books and articles on the problems of conceptualizing and measuring power and influence. While most of these do not deal explicitly with city politics, those interested in community power may find this section a useful resource.

Other Bibliographies Related to the Study of Community Power

Beck, Carl and J. Thomas McKechnie, *Political Elites, A Select Computerized Bibliography* (Cambridge: M.I.T. Press, 1968).

Although the primary focus of this bibliography is the study of political elites in comparative politics, it does include extensive citations of studies of community power structure. The first section is a listing of citations on the basis of key words in title. Among key words included are "community," "structure" and "power." The time period covered is 1945-mid-1967.

Bell, Wendell, Richard J. Hill and Charles R. Wright, *Public Leadership* (San Francisco: Chandler Publishing Co., 1961) pp. 196-228.
  This is a selected bibliography (not annotated) of books, articles, and unpublished documents on public leadership jn the United States.

Gilbert, Claire, "The Study of Community Power: A Summary and a Test," in Scott Greer, et. al., eds., *The New Urbanization* (New York: St. Martin's Press, 1968) pp. 222-45.
  This article includes an extensive bibliography of community power studies. The listings are not annotated.

Keynes, Edward and David M. Ricci, eds., *Political Power, Community and Democracy* (Chicago: Rand McNally & Co., 1970).
  "Selected Bibliography of Community Power and Related Subjects," prepared with the assistance of Gary W. Sykes, pp. 255-77.
  Some of these items are annotated.

Norval, Glenn D., Jon P. Alston and David Weiner, *Social Stratification: A Research Bibliography* (Berkeley, California: The Glendessary Press, Inc., 1970).
  This bibliography is divided into two sections. Part I deals with "Social Stratification" and Part II with "Social Mobility and the Correlates of Stratification." Within Part I is a section entitled "Power, Authority and Leadership at the Community Level." The authors acknowledge drawing almost exclusively on Pellegrin's bibliography in the *Southwestern Social Science Quarterly*. In addition to this section, there are three others on power, authority and leadership – general treatments, the national level and specific treatments. None of the citations are annotated.

Pellegrin, Ronald J., "Selected Bibliography on Community Power Structure," *Southwestern Social Science Quarterly* 48 (December 1967) 451-65. The items here are not annotated.

Press, Charles, *Main Street Politics: Policy Making at the Local Level. A Survey of the Periodical Literature since 1950* (East Lansing: Michigan State University, 1962.)
  This is an annotated bibliography comprised primarily of journal articles related to community power and to community politics in general, which appeared (for the most part) between 1951 and 1961. Following a short preface which reviews major themes, the bibliography is divided into sections on (1) community power, (2) major actors, (3) power logic, and (4) study and application. A separate bibliography of books and pamphlets (not annotated) is included, as is a list of other bibliographies.

Acknowledgements

A number of scholars who have written on the subject of community power provided us with advice and assistance and without them this bibliography would not be as comprehensive as it is. We are especially grateful to John Bunzel, Claire Gilbert, Floyd Hunter, Nelson Polsby and Frederick Wirt. We are in debt also to John Geesman and Evelyn Mercer, who undertook the tiresome task of double-checking the citations for accuracy, and Susan Fergenson, who provided substantial assistance on the composition of the final manuscript. The Institute of Governmental Studies at the University of California, Berkeley, supported an initial draft of this bibliography and that aid is much appreciated.

Chapter 1

AN HISTORICAL OVERVIEW OF THE STUDY OF
COMMUNITY POWER

Willis D. Hawley

Contemporary interest in the study of community power appears to have its origins in a handful of community studies done during the 1920's and 1930's. The most notable, and in many ways the most influential, of these studies were the Middletown studies of Robert S. and Helen M. Lynd.[1] Following World War II, more scholars entered the vineyards and in 1953 the publication of Floyd Hunter's *Community Power Structure*[2] signaled the full-scale assault on the subject. Most studies, especially those which received much notoriety, concluded that the social, economic, and political life of American communities was dominated by a relatively small group of wealthy and/or socially prestigious individuals whose values were more or less congruent and who were not, for the most part, accountable to the citizens of the communities they controlled.

Most of the research on community power prior to 1960 was conducted by social anthropologists and, especially, sociologists rather than political scientists or economists. The early dominance of the field by sociologists may be explained by a number of factors. First, with few exceptions, political scientists who worked in community settings tended to define politics somewhat narrowly and characteristically focused their attention on the form and structure of city and county governmental institutions.[3] Second, the study of local politics did not hold much

---

[1] *Middletown* (New York: Harcourt, Brace and Co., 1929); *Middletown in Transition* (New York: Harcourt, Brace and Co., 1937).

[2] *Community Power Structure* (Chapel Hill: University of North Carolina Press, 1953).

[3] See Lawrence Herson, "The Lost World of Municipal Government," *American Political Science Review* 51 (June 1957) 330-45.

status within the profession of political science and the research techniques and strategies of the so-called behavioral approach to politics[4] — which were necessary to the systematic analysis of community power — had not been widely adopted, especially by political scientists familiar with local affairs. Third, the training and background of many sociologists who studied community power led them to a conflict interpretation of social order and an interest in structural-functionalism. Thus, sociologists may have been more sensitive than political scientists to normative social theories and to ways of conceptualizing social systems which resulted in their considering community study significant for analyzing society.[5]

Beginning in the mid-1950's, both the findings and the research strategies of these earlier studies were subjected to increasingly severe criticism, especially from political scientists. But not until 1960 did a number of studies begin to appear which operationalized alternative methodologies and furnished empirical evidence for the argument that community power in America was more often than not shared by elites with varying interests and that no one set of elites or no one person — unless, perhaps, it was the chief elected official — played a significant role in more than one or two issue areas. The most influential studies published at the outset of this decade were *Governing New York City,* by Wallace S. Sayre and Herbert Kaufman, Robert Dahl's *Who Governs?* and Edward Banfield's *Political Influence.*[6]

A considerable amount of the material published on community power during the early 1960's was heavily oriented toward the resolution of methodological problems though behind much of this putatively technical debate lay conflicting assumptions about the character of American politics.[7]

---

[4] See Robert Dahl, "The Behavioral Approach to Politics: Epitaph for a Monument to a Successful Protest," *American Political Science Review* 55 (December 1961) 763-72.

[5] This point was initially brought to my attention by Steven Blutza. On some aspects of this point see Nelson Polsby, *Community Power and Political Theory* (New Haven: Yale University Press, 1963).

[6] *Governing New York City* (New York: Russell Sage Foundation, 1960), *Who Governs?* (New Haven: Yale University Press, 1961) and *Political Influence* (New York: The Free Press, 1961).

[7] Many of the most important field studies focused substantial attention on the advantages and disadvantages of alternative methodologies. See for example, Aaron Wildavsky, *Leadership in a Small Town* (Totowa, N.J.: Bedminster Press, 1964); Robert Presthus, *Men at the Top* (New York: Oxford University Press, 1964); and Linton C. Freeman, et. al., "Locating Leaders in Local Communities: A Comparison of Some Alternative Approaches," *American Sociological Review* 28 (October 1963) 791-98. (Wildavsky and Presthus were concerned about a number of questions in addition to methodology.) The debate among some students of community power over appropriate research procedures has been particularly intense. Some of the flavor of this argument

Almost all of the studies of community power that appeared before the mid-1960's were limited in their scope to one or two communities though much of the evaluative literature argued that we were not likely to learn much more about community power in the absence of more sophisticated comparative research. As Peter Rossi observed: "Each author owns his own town, defending it from the erroneous and somewhat heretical conceptualizations of others, much the way a feudal lord defends the integrity of the local patron saint against the false counterclaims of nearby realms."[8]

In 1964, *The Rulers and the Ruled* by Robert Agger, Marshall Goldstein and Bert Swanson appeared suggesting, by illustration, the importance of multi-community longitudinal study.[9] While there are obvious advantages of research of this type, the enormous costs in commitment, money and time that are so apparent in the work of Agger and his associates explain why more such studies have not been undertaken.

The interest in comparative community power studies that began to find its way into print in the mid-sixties was accompanied by a number of efforts to synthesize systematically the results of other studies and to develop the bases of a theory of community power therefrom.[10]

One of the greatest gaps in the literature on community power is the impact that extra-community forces — especially county, state and federal governments — have on local patterns of decision making. There have been a number of efforts to specify the role that external economic factors play in community politics, but systematic research on the linkages between what have been called the vertical and horizontal axes of community power has yet to be reported.[11]

---

can be tested economically by examining a series of articles by Polsby, Wolfinger, Erickson, Ehrlich, and D'Antonio which appeared in Volume 27 (1962) of the *American Sociological Review*.

[8] Peter Rossi, "Power and Community Structure," *Midwest Journal of Political Science* 4 (November 1960) 390-401.

[9] (New York: John Wiley and Sons, 1964).

[10] Among those who have engaged most profitably in such secondary analyses and theory building are Terry Clark, Claire Gilbert and John Walton. See Terry Clark, ed., *Community Structure and Decision-Making* (San Francisco: Chandler Publishing Co., 1968); and David Rogers, "Community Political Systems: A Framework and Hypothesis for Comparative Studies" in Bert E. Swanson, ed., *Current Trends in Comparative Community Studies* (Kansas City: Community Studies, Inc., 1962), pp. 31-48.

[11] Cf. Roland L. Warren, *The Community in America* (Chicago: Rand McNally, 1963). One of the most comprehensive efforts to identify these relationships remains Arthur Vidich and Joseph Bensman, *Small Town in Mass Society* (Princeton: Princeton University Press, 1958.)

In recent years the number of case studies and intensive analyses of individual communities has been relatively small. At the same time, however, a number of scholars have begun, for the first time, to examine the structure of community decision making in other than American communities.[12]

The apparent decline in the volume of studies of community power does not reflect — judging by the growing number of anthologies on the subject[13] and the continuing output of analyses of previous studies[14] — a decline of interest in community power structure. Rather, it may be that the immense conceptual and methodological difficulties on the one hand, and low theoretical yield of prior studies on the other, has discouraged the proliferation of efforts at extensive field research. Moreover, the last three or four years has seen a dramatic growth of interest on the part of scholars in the analysis of public policy at the local level.[15]

Up to the present time, few studies of community power have devoted much attention to policy makers. (Some notable exceptions to this are the writings of Amos Hawley, Terry Clark and Francine Rabinovitz.)[16] Despite the paucity of past attempts to link the study of community power to policy analysis, it seems unlikely that much future research on community power will proceed without a strong emphasis on the policy consequences of different patterns of decision making. In the first place, as implied above, the normative concerns of persons interested in urban research have shifted from primarily philosophical or institutional analysis, to

---

[12] Almost all of the studies of communities in other countries that have been published in English have appeared since 1967. See, for example, Delbert C. Miller, *International Community Power Structures* (Bloomington: Indiana University Press, 1970).

[13] For example, Willis D. Hawley and Frederick Wirt, eds., *The Search for Community Power* (Englewood Cliffs, N.J.: Prentice-Hall, Inc., 1968); Terry Clark, ed., *op. cit.;* Edward Keynes and David Ricci, eds., *Political Power, Community and Democracy* (Chicago: Rand McNally, 1970); and Michael Aiken and Paul E. Mott, eds., *The Structure of Community Power* (New York: Random House, 1970).

[14] See, for example, Thomas Dye, "Community Power Studies" in James A. Robinson, ed., *Political Science Annual; Volume II-1969* (Indianapolis and New York: Bobbs-Merrill Co., Inc., 1970), pp. 35-71; and David Ricci, *Community Power and Democratic Theory: The Logic of Political Analysis* (New York: Random House, 1971).

[15] See, for example, James Q. Wilson, ed., *City Politics and Public Policy* (New York: John Wiley & Sons, 1969); Brett Hawkins, *Politics and Urban Policies* (Indianapolis: Bobbs-Merrill, 1971); and Willis D. Hawley, *The Partisan Bias of Non-Partisanship* (New York: John Wiley, forthcoming), Ch. 6 and the sources cited there.

[16] See Amos Hawley, "Community Power and Urban Renewal Success," *American Journal of Sociology* 68 (June 1963) 422-31; Terry N. Clark, "Community

policy studies. James Q. Wilson explains this development when he says: "'Who Governs?' is an interesting and important question; an even more interesting and more important question, . . . is 'what *difference* does it make who governs?'"[17]

A second and more pragmatic reason why future research on community power is likely to have a policy emphasis is that such inquiry is very costly and the sources of financial support for urban research are primarily concerned with social change rather than with issues of democratic theory or social science methodology.

While the literature on community power is extensive, the power arrangements in only a fraction of American communities have been subjected to systematic investigation by social scientists. Moreover, the communities studied by no means represent a cross-section of American communities. For example, it appears that most research has been carried out in towns and cities which are outside the direct influence of metropolitan centers,[18] although less than a third of the nation's people live in such communities. It also seems that western and southwestern cities are underrepresented. Further, it may be that towns and cities within the direct cultural influence of colleges and universities are overrepresented.

In any case, the extent to which the cities and towns studied are "unrepresentative," and the impact this may have on the images we have of community power in America, seem to warrant investigation.

When one looks back over the numerous community studies, it appears that the results of earlier studies have indicated that community power was more highly concentrated than has recent research. This difference is often explained by observing that research methods are becoming more sophisticated and that we are more aware now of the complexity and subtleties of community power. While this explanation seems reasonable, it may also be that power in many American communities is, generally, becoming more diffused.

Walton has noted that studies of thirty-two cities show that when changes in the "power structure" occur, the "structure" invariably becomes more dispersed.[19]

Structure, Decision Making, Budget Expenditures and Urban Renewal in 51 American Communities," in Frederick M. Wirt, ed., *Future Directions in Community Power Research: A Colloquium* (Berkeley: Institute of Governmental Studies, Univ. of Calif., 1971); and Francine Rabinovitz, *City Politics and Planning* (New York: Atherton Press, 1969).

[17] James Q. Wilson, "We Need to Shift Focus," in Edward H. Buchrig, ed., *Essays in Political Science* (Bloomington: Indiana University Press, 1966), pp. 131.

[18] Walton determined that in the studies he was able to identify thirty-six out of forty-eight cities were "independent" rather than "satellites" of a central city (or presumably the metropolitan center itself); "Differential Patterns of Community Power Structure: An Explanation Based on Interdependence," in Terry N. Clark, ed., *op. cit.*, pp. 441-59.

[19] Walton, *op. cit.*

Claire Gilbert has examined the reports on studies conducted in 166 American communities. Comparing the findings of earlier with more recent research she concluded:

> The evidence supports the notion that increasing scale of society is reflected in the political structure of local communities. It appears that power — i.e., the ability to make binding decisions for the community — is less and less in the hands of a privileged few and is increasingly dependent upon the broker, be he elected official or not, who can bring together (to the extent he can bring together) the various elements in the *community*.[20]

The most extensive research and analysis of community power and its consequences underway at the end of 1971 was that being directed and coordinated by Terry Clark and by other scholars associated with the International Sociological Association Committee on Community Research (CCR).[21] Under Clark's direction, the International Studies of Values in Politics program and the National Opinion Research Center at the University of Chicago are examining patterns of decision making and their consequences in fifty-one American communities. Clark's research seeks to link together the structural characteristics of communities, decision-making structures and policy outputs.[22]

The study of community power has engaged the energies of some of America's most prestigious social scientists and it has yielded some important insights to the debate over democratic theory, it has advanced the development of more sophisticated research methodologies, it has provided substantial information about how local political systems operate, and it has furthered our understanding of leadership. Nevertheless, given the talent and energies that have been devoted to the enterprise, we seem to be some distance from developing a theory of community power. That is, while some impressive exploratory work has been done we still do not have any very clear ideas about the factors that might account for variations in the patterns of power distribution in American (or any other) communities. This observation concerning the relatively low theoretical yield of the study of community power applies, of course, to many areas of social science research.

---

[20] Claire Gilbert, "Community Power and Decision Making: A Quantitative Examination of Previous Research," in Terry N. Clark, ed., *Community Structure and Decision-Making*, pp. 139-58.

[21] The first results of the CCR's efforts will appear in 1972 in a collection of articles edited by Terry Clark, ed., *Comparative Community Politics* (forthcoming).

[22] For a brief description of this research see Terry Clark, ed., *Community Structure and Decision-Making*, pp. 463-78. One important article based on this study is Clark's "Community Structure, Decision Making, Budget Expenditures and Urban Renewal in 51 Communities," *op. cit.*

Indeed, it may be that we know more about the factors that shape community decision-making patterns than we do about decision making in other political arenas.

Perhaps the reason why, at least through 1970, community power research has yielded less than one might have hoped for is that the inquiry, in general, has proceeded without a widely accepted paradigm which might have ordered, and facilitated the comparability of, the numerous studies. As Thomas Kuhn has noted, "In the absence of a paradigm, or some candidate for a paradigm, all the facts that could possibly pertain to the development of a given science [here a branch of science] are likely to seem equally relevant. As a result, early fact gathering is a far more nearly random activity than the one that subsequent scientific development makes familiar."[23]

Recently, substantial progress has been made in developing a set of conventions to guide community power research.[24] However, before these important steps in theory building can be taken, it appears that certain key problems require more specific, though not necessarily definitive, answers.

First, there is a need to develop some consensus about how power will be defined and operationally measured. This will not be easy: it is a problem that students of politics have wrestled with since Plato considered the matter.[25] While efforts to resolve this problem are being made, it may suffice for students of community power to be explicit about the definition of power which guided their research and the way they operationalized that conceptualization. It seems quite clear, however, that notions of power which focus attention solely, or even primarily, on the resolution of issues that are dealt with by the formal institutions of government are inadequate.

Second, the tiresome but important debate about appropriate research strategies requires resolution beyond the present agreement that no one technique will suffice. It is not clear, for example, what the reputational approach (the identification of influentials by "knowledgeable" people in the community), which

---

[23] Thomas Kuhn, *The Structure of Scientific Revolutions* (Chicago: University of Chicago Press, 1962), p. 15.

[24] See, for example, Terry N. Clark, "Power and Community Structure: Who Governs Where and When," in Charles Bonjean, Terry N. Clark, and Robert L. Lineberry, eds., *Community Politics* (New York: Free Press, 1971), pp. 174-87; and Michael Aiken, "The Distribution of Community Power: Structural Bases and Social Consequences," in Aiken and Mott, *op. cit.*, 487-525.

[25] For a succinct summary of some of the many problems involved see James March, "The Power of Power," in David Easton, ed., *Varieties of Political Theories* (Englewood Cliffs, N.J.: Prentice-Hall, Inc., 1966), pp. 39-70.

continues to be the most widely employed methodology, really tells us. Since reputation is a power resource, the reputational approach tells us something about the potential power individuals or groups might mobilize. It is less certain whether this approach allows us to specify the scope of potential power (even within issue areas) or the probabilities that such power will be utilized. Earlier studies employing both reputational and decision-making methods showed poor correlations between the patterns of influence that emerged from each research strategy. What is needed is a multidimensional methodology for identifying political influentials that specifies the relative validity to be placed on the data derived from different techniques.

Third, it is necessary to develop more fully a conceptualization of the relationship between community structure and participation in community decision making as these relate to the distribution of power.

Fourth, there is a need to specify a minimum set of variables whose consequences for the distribution of power researchers might investigate. Such variables would include situational, cultural, structural and environmental factors that might hypothetically affect the distribution of power.[26]

Finally, the study of community power and policy analysis need to be linked not only because it is normatively important to do so or because research resources may be contingent on such a merger. The linkage is important to the development of the descriptive theory since policy outcomes may provide clues to the distribution of influence and sometimes redefine the rules of the game that constrain the use of power resources.[27]

The relationship between patterns of community power and policy outputs can be derived only if it is studied in a number of different issue areas. And if such efforts are to have much theoretical yield, the differing results that are likely to emerge can be linked to (1) some common characteristics of different substantive policies and (2) the role that different types of policy arenas play in maintaining or altering the structure of political systems.[28]

---

[26] Important steps in meeting this need have been made by Terry Clark, Michael Aiken and Robert Alford. See footnote 24 above and Michael Aiken and Robert Alford, "Community Structure and Innovation: Public Housing, Urban Renewal, and the War on Poverty," in Terry N. Clark, ed., *Comparative Community Politics,* forthcoming.

[27] See Andrew McFarland, *Power and Leadership in Pluralist Systems* (Stanford: Stanford University Press, 1969), Ch. 5. However, power cannot be determined by resting our analysis solely on the discovery of who benefits in a political system. Some of the reasons for this are outlined by Nelson Polsby, *Community Power and Political Theory, op. cit.*

[28] See, for example, Theodore Lowi, "American Business, Public Policy, Case Studies, and Political Theory," *World Politics* 16 (July 1964) pp. 677-715.

These are not the only issues that need to be resolved before a theory of community power can be formulated and empirically tested but they are some of the first items that ought to be on the agenda of would-be theory builders.

It is our hope that this volume will, among other things, ease the task of those who seek to develop the theory or theories that might explain the sources and consequences of different patterns of power and community decision making.

Terry Clark, in an unpublished paper entitled "The Structure of Community Influence," (1972) suggests that different patterns in the allocation of power resources can be linked consistently to policy consequences if a distinction is made between policies that involve public or indivisible goods (financial administration and general control) and those that involve "separable" goods (police, fire and sanitation).

Chapter 2

FIELD STUDIES OF COMMUNITIES FOCUSING ON THE
DISTRIBUTION OF INFLUENCE

Abu-Laban, Baha. "Social Origins and Occupational Career Patterns of Community Leaders," *Sociological Inquiry* 33 (Spring 1963) 131-40.

The materials on which the findings are based were collected beginning in 1959 in "Pacific Town," Washington (population 5,000.) A panel of twelve community "knowledgeables," representative of various institutional sectors in the community, was invited to identify the "most important and influential" leaders in Pacific Town. The twenty-five persons named most often were designated as "probable community leaders" and were interviewed. Each of them was requested to add other names if necessary to the primary list of leaders. As a result of this second level of leadership nomination three new persons were incorporated into the leadership pool. The twenty-eight persons were then asked to rank the ten most influential persons on the list of leaders. These ten were identified as the top leaders.

The author concludes that the social origins of the Pacific Town leaders generally parallel the findings in other research. All of the leaders identified were men recruited from high-ranking positions in business and industry, banking, insurance, local government, the professions, and in educational and civic sectors. They were characterized by: (1) relatively high educational attainment; (2) long residence in the community; (3) active participation in voluntary associations and (4) being predominantly older in age.

It is also concluded that those who may assume leadership functions are characterized by occupational career patterns reflecting upper mobility, stability and success. The author suggests that further research relating the motivational structure of leaders to an empirical typology of leaders based on their occupational career patterns might be fruitful and that comparative research is needed to determine under what conditions certain types of life careers are likely to be represented in the community leadership structure.

Adrian, Charles R. "Leadership and Decision Making in Manager Cities: A Study of Three Communities," *Public Administration Review* 18 (Summer 1958) 208-13.

In three middle-sized Michigan cities, ranging in population from 50,000 to 80,000, city managers and their chief assistants were seen as the major source of policy innovation and leadership in the city government. All of the cities conducted nonpartisan elections for city councilmen. Councilmen seldom assumed leadership on important issues and seemed reluctant to risk the political consequences of such initiative. On non-governmental matters, voluntary associations exercised the dominant leadership and influence.

Agger, Robert E., and Goldrich, Daniel. "Community Power Structures and Partisanship," *American Sociological Review* 23 (August 1958) 383-92.

Political structure and participation are compared in two small Oregon communities ("Valley City," population 2,000 adults and "Boom Town," total population 16,000). A randomly selected sample of residents in each community and its fringe area was asked to identify community leaders. Participant observers also evaluated the leadership role of potential influentials. The power structure in Valley City was dominated by three individuals who held, or had held, key political offices. Power in Boom Town is seen as polynucleated.

In both communities Republicans dominated the voluntary associations. In the larger of the two communities, however, Democrats obtained leadership in community affairs through participation in their political party or directly in local government. In Valley City, Republicans dominated all aspects of community policy making. Among the factors contributing to more influence of Democrats in Boom Town were the diffusion of power which allowed for greater access for positions of influence for those with moderate power resources, and the different nature of the issues with which the two communities were concerned.

Agger, Robert E.; Goldrich, Daniel; and Swanson, Bert E. *The Rulers and the Ruled: Political Power and Impotence in American Communities* (New York: John Wiley and Sons, Inc., 1964).

Reviews:

Eulau, Heinz, *American Political Science Review* 58 (December 1964) 972-73.

Nimmo, Dan, *Journal of Politics* 27 (February 1965) 235-36.

Smith, Paul A., *Midwest Journal of Political Science* 9 (February 1965) 112-14.

Kellstadt, Lyman, "Atlanta to Oretown: Identifying Community Elites," *Public Administration Review* 25 (June 1965) 161-68.

Bell, Wendell, *American Sociological Review* 30 (June 1965) 435-36.

Cutright, Phillips, *American Journal of Sociology* 70 (January 1965) 488.

Auerbach, A.J., *Administrative Science Quarterly* 10 (September 1965) 276-78.

Walter, Benjamin, *Social Forces* 43 (May 1965) 592-94.

The data on which this volume is based were collected from two western and two southern communities which varied in size from 2,000 to 100,000. These communities were studied by the authors over an extended period of time (about five years in the case of the southern communities and almost ten years in the case of the western communities). Random samples of citizens and leaders were interviewed. The decision-making process itself was observed and newspapers and other records were carefully examined.

The authors found that the distribution of influence is somewhat different in each of these communities and that it tended to vary within each community over time. From their empirical findings, the authors construct a series of propositions and theoretical assumptions. The authors suggest that communities may be classified in terms of the relationship between the community power structure (the distribution of political power among citizens and the ideology of political leaders) and political regimes. "Political regime" is defined as the probability of illegitimate sanctions blocking efforts to shift the scope of government and the sense of electoral potency on the part of the citizenry; in other words, the rules of the game by which decision making is carried out in a given community. The authors also suggest additional dimensions by which one might modify and proliferate simple typologies into multi-faceted models to fit a range of real world situations.

The book also contains a critical analysis of existing studies on community power, as well as an appendix in which the concepts developed in the book are applied in a speculative way to an abstract analysis of big city political systems.

Agger, Robert E., and Ostrom, Vincent. "The Political Structure of the Small Community," *Public Opinion Quarterly* 20 (Spring 1956) 81-89.

A random sample of 260 persons in a small rural community in the western states (population 3,000) is asked to identify political leaders in the community. It was found that persons with different rates of political participation tended to identify different persons as leaders. Three key individuals are identified along with a few other men who made up the top leadership group. All either held, or had held political office and all were active in politics. The top leaders were of relatively high socioeconomic status, although they were not business leaders. Business leaders were beginning to challenge the position of the top leadership group. The leadership group was fairly well integrated but was apparently responsive to a somewhat representative group of subleaders. The authors identify five political roles in the community: (1) "Advisors," persons from whom others seek advice (8 percent of the adult population); (2) "Talkers," policy matter discussants (14 percent); (3) "Listeners," informed but passive participants in the political process (13 percent); (4) "Workers" (9 percent) and (5) "Nonparticipants" (51 percent).

Note: (Another version of this study appears under the title "Political Participation in a Small Community," in Heinz Eulau et. al, eds., *Political Behavior* (New York: The Free Press, 1961) pp. 138-48.

Alford, Robert R. "Bureaucracy and Participation in Four Wisconsin Cities," *Urban Affairs Quarterly* 5 (September 1969) 5-30.

This article is a condensed version of a book cited below.

Alford, Robert R., *Bureaucracy and Participation: Political Cultures in Four Wisconsin Cities* (Chicago: Rand McNally and Co., 1969).

Reviews:

Wilson, James Q., *American Political Science Review* 64 (March 1970) 198.

Wirt, Frederick M., *American Sociological Review* 35 (December 1970) 1106-7.

Schaffer, Albert, *Social Forces* 48 (June 1970) 548-49.

This study probes the relationship between (1) the nature of political decision making — operationalized in terms of the degree of bureaucracy and the level of group and individual participation, (2) the social and economic structure of the community, and (3) the direction of public policies. Four middle-sized Wisconsin cities provide the study sites and a variety of types of data, including evidence derived from systematic elite and citizen surveys, are collated and analyzed. Alford concludes that cities in which political decision making is highly bureaucratic and participatory (categorized as modern) are: (1) likely to experience more professional public service and (2) likely to receive more aid support from national and state governments (e.g. urban renewal and anti-poverty programs).

Differences in the political cultures of the cities studied do not appear to be traceable to the differences in the attitudes of the people other than those differences in attitudes that can be accounted for by the religion or social class of his respondents.

Bachrach, Peter, and Baratz, Morton S., *Power and Poverty: Theory and Practice* (New York: Oxford University Press, 1970).

Drawing upon a case study of the anti-poverty program in Baltimore and their earlier writings — "The Two Faces of Power" and "Decisions and Nondecisions: An Analytical Framework" which are reprinted here — the authors elaborate a model of the political process. The model focuses on the conflict between groups seeking reallocation of values and those committed to existing values. Central to the model are the barriers to change at different levels of the decision and nondecision-making process.

In their analysis of poverty, race and politics in Baltimore, the authors find that the history of the anti-poverty program is divided into two periods. In the first, power was primarily exercised in the form of nondecisions which supported a system that prevented the demands of certain groups in the community from being heard. In the second period, ideological and institutional changes of considerable magnitude were brought about by those who, although previously excluded from the political system, were strengthened by power resources supplied by the federal government. Black leaders, through a show of force rather than through the voluntary decision of the white majority, won meaningful involvement in shaping policies that affect their community.

Bachrach, Peter. "A Power Analysis: The Shaping of Antipoverty Policy in Baltimore," *Public Policy* 18 (Winter 1970) 155-86.

This article was re-worked for inclusion in Bachrach and Baratz, *Power and Poverty* (1970).

Bailey, Norman A. "Local and Community Power in Angola," *Western Political Quarterly* 21 (September 1968) 400-408.

In a trip to Africa in 1965, the author tested two propositions concerning the political process in an authoritarian society. These were (1) the political process in authoritarian societies is identical with that of democratic societies with the exception of the power of bloc voting in the latter, as distinct from totalitarian regimes in which competition is destroyed, and (2) in authoritarian societies the state (government and bureaucracy) is clearly seen as a distinct power aggregate different in function but not in kind from other power aggregates operating in society and engaged in the political process. These propositions were tested by use of a decision-making study of two decisions and involved interviewing government officials, legislative representatives and private individuals. The results outlined were checked by a rudimentary reputational analysis and by study of the nominating process for legislative councils. The investigation produced evidence of interest group articulation and effective popular pressure and, also, of intra-state pluralism among different levels of government. The findings support, in the author's opinion, the validity of the hypothetical propositions set forth at the beginning.

Baltzell, E. Digby. *Philadelphia Gentlemen, The Making of a National Upper Class* (Glencoe, Illinois: The Free Press, 1958).
Reviews:
Miller, William, *American Sociological Review* 23 (August 1958) 451-52.

Utilizing the *Philadelphia Social Register* and *Who's Who in America*, Baltzell identifies 226 Philadelphians who in 1940 were both socially elite and occupationally high placed. This group comprises, for the author, an "American Business Aristocracy." Among the 226 persons identified, a little less than a fourth of these are singled out as being the most influential. He argues that these persons are the ruling class in Philadelphia, and he examines in detail their family background, religious affiliation, educational experiences, and associational memberships, as well as their role and that of their families in the areas of politics, journalism, business and finance and civic affairs.

The author refers only infrequently to the relationship between the influence of this business aristocracy in the Philadelphia area and its influence in the seats of national power. The relationship between the Philadelphia business aristocracy and the holders of positions of political influence in government, such as elected officials and party workers, is not made clear. The ways in which the "Philadelphia gentlemen" shape public policy and to what ends is not dealt with explicitly.

Banfield, Edward C. *Big City Politics* (New York: Random House, 1965).
Reviews:
Press, Charles, *Midwest Journal of Political Science* 10 (May 1966) 248-50.

The author analyzes the character and workings of the political systems in nine American cities: Atlanta, Boston, Detroit, El Paso, Los Angeles, Miami, Philadelphia, St. Louis and Seattle. The data upon which much of the analysis is based were compiled by a number of different scholars under the sponsorship of the Joint Center for Urban Studies of the Massachusetts Institute of Technology and Harvard University. (The report of each of these scholars was published separately by the Center.) Banfield organizes his analysis around six key concerns: (1) population and economy; (2) how the government is organized; (3) "how it really works"; (4) how politicians get elected; (5) interest groups and influentials and (6) how issues are handled.

Banfield, Edward C. *Political Influence* (Glencoe, Illinois: The Free Press, 1961).
   Reviews:
      Segrest, Earl C., *Western Political Quarterly* 17 (March 1964) 134-36.
      Peabody, Robert L., *Public Opinion Quarterly* 26 (Spring 1962) 153-54.
      Janowitz, Morris, *Public Opinion Quarterly* 26 (Fall 1962) 398-410.

The author investigates the way in which the outcome of six major civic issues in Chicago was determined. On the basis of his thorough examination of the decision-making process in these key areas, the author concludes that there is no ruling elite in Chicago and he explains in some detail why economic dominants do not dominate decision making in Chicago. He concludes that influence in community affairs varies with the issue, and that issues tend to rise out of the maintenance and enhancement needs of large formal organizations. Great emphasis is placed on the integrative functions of the political party and on the central role of the mayor of Chicago in the decision-making process, especially under the administration of Mayor Richard Daley. The decision-making process is characterized as one in which action is taken only when political risks for the actors, and the mayor in particular, are minimal.

Barth, Ernest A. T. "Community Influence Systems: Structure and Change," *Social Forces* 40 (October 1961) 58-63.

The structure of influence is studied in six small communities. Community influentials are identified in each community by a panel of "knowledgeables." The distribution of influence seemed to vary among communities and the author types this variation as follows: pyramidal, clique based, truncated pyramid, and disorganized influence. He suggests that more diffused patterns of political influence are associated with a rapid rate of urban growth and a high rate of absentee ownership of industry.

Barth, Ernest A. T., and Abu-Laban, Baha. "Power Structure and the Negro Sub-community," *American Sociological Review* 24 (February 1959) 69-76.

This study is conceived as a replication of Floyd Hunter's study of the power relationship between Negroes and Whites in Atlanta. The study is undertaken in "Pacific City" (Seattle, Washington) and the conclusions are based on information obtained from a panel of judges who were themselves nominated by another panel of "knowledgeables." The pattern of influence in the Negro sub-community is seen as fluid and unstable as compared to that in Atlanta and the leaders are likely to hold positions in civil rights protest organizations, rather than in the business and commercial organizations as in Atlanta. The Negro sub-community is seen as having no serious influence on the decisions made in a larger community of Seattle.

Belknap, George M., and Smuckler, Ralph. "Political Power Relations in a Mid-West City," *Public Opinion Quarterly* 20 (Spring 1956) 73-81.

Based on interviews with 103 residents of a Michigan city of 50,000, and an additional fifty-six "actives" who are identified from a number of different sources, the authors conclude that a small number (10-15) of individuals possesses influence over, and initiates action on, most community issues. Most of these "top influentials" have not held public office. A second echelon of leadership, involving about sixty persons and which varies in composition according to the issue, is identified. The mass public remains indifferent or unresponsive to the activities of both leadership groups. Different persons seem to exercise influence on local, state, and national affairs.

It is noted that "nonactives" were much more inclined than actives to identify holders of public office as the most influential. The different characteristics of actives and inactives are also analyzed.

Note: An earlier version of this article appeared under the title *Leadership and Participation in Urban Political Affairs* (East Lansing: Government Research Bureau, Michigan State University, 1956). This pamphlet makes essentially the same points made in the article discussed immediately above.

Belknap, Ivan, and Steile, John. *The Community and Its Hospitals* (Syracuse, N.Y.: Syracuse University Press, 1963).

Reviews:
Elling, Ray H., *Administrative Science Quarterly* 8 (March 1964) 564-66.
Maney, Ann C., *Social Forces* 42 (March 1964) 387-88.

Birch, A.H. *Smalltown Politics: A Study of Political Life in Glossop* (London: Oxford University Press, 1959).

In this study of Glossop, England, population 18,000, the author examines the nature of the political system in substantial depth. Various research methods are employed including elite interviews, a random sample survey of the citizenry, and the examination of documentary and journalistic materials. He examines the historical context of contemporary politics and how the development of economic interdependence with other communities, the growth of governmental functions at the national and county level, and the changing social structure of the town have shaped the manner and pattern of political decision making.

Blasier, Cole. "Power and Social Change in Colombia: The Cauca Valley," *Journal of Inter-American Studies* 8 (July 1966) 386-410.

Bloomberg, Warner, Jr.; Sunshine, Morris H.; and Fararo, Thomas J. *Suburban Power Structures in Public Education: A Study of Values, Influence, and Tax Effort* (Syracuse, New York: Syracuse University Press, 1963).

This study of the structure of influence in four suburbs of Syracuse focuses on the question of why public education in some communities is better financed than others. Community leaders are identified both by nomination and through their actual participation in public decision making. The authors find that the leadership pools discovered by each of these two methods is somewhat different. They conclude that leadership in each of the suburbs is specialized in terms of given types of issues.

Bohlen, J. M., et al. *A Comparative Analysis of Community Power Structures* (Ames, Iowa: Iowa State University, *Rural Sociology Report,* No. 50, 1967).

Bonjean, Charles M. "Community Leadership: A Case Study and Conceptual Refinement," *American Journal of Sociology* 68 (May 1963) 672-81.

This article is seen by the author as an answer to the numerous criticisms of the reputational approach to the study of community power. In a study of Burlington, North Carolina, population 33,000, a "knowledgeable" person was asked to nominate "those who really get things done." These persons were then interviewed and they were asked to nominate community leaders. Persons continued to be interviewed until new interviews failed to yield new information. Forty-five persons were then interviewed. The rankings were weighed according to the relative influence attributed and a list of sixteen leaders was ultimately formulated. The sixteen reputed leaders in turn were asked to evaluate their own role in decision making in community affairs and the role of others who were nominated as leaders. Three types of leaders were thereby identified: (1) "Visible Leaders," those who are perceived by both "knowledgeables" and top leaders as influential; (2) "Concealed Leaders," persons who are ranked high in influence by the nominated leaders but who are not perceived as leaders by the "knowledgeables" and (3) "Symbolic Leaders," those who are perceived by the "knowledgeables" as influential but who are not seen as powerful by the nominated leaders, i.e., those in the best position to know.

The author concludes, ". . . Burlington's leadership structure may be seen as a network of overlapping subgroups, some visible and some concealed, coordinated by one central visible figure."

Bonjean, Charles M., and Carter, Lewis F. "Legitimacy and Visibility: Leadership Structures Related to Four Community Systems," *Pacific Sociological Review* 8 (Spring 1965) 16-20.

Presumably "knowledgeable" persons in each of four communities in North Carolina were asked to identify community leaders. The identified community leaders are then asked to identify other leaders and to evaluate their own position in community affairs. The power structures of these communities are seen by the authors as varying in terms of visibility (the degree to which community members are aware who decision-makers are) and legitimacy (the degree to which decision-makers hold formal positions in the political and associational structure of the community). Those community characteristics most closely associated with a covert-type power structure were: high rates of population growth, high proportions of low-income and dependent persons in the population, and lesser degrees of social, economic and governmental complexity. The variability in the legitimacy of the leadership structure was restricted, but in general the factors related to visibility were also related to legitimacy.

Bonjean, Charles M. "Class Status and Power Reputation," *Sociology and Social Research* 49 (October 1964) 69-75.

Utilizing data developed in a study of four North Carolina communities of varying sizes, the author identifies leaders as: (1) visible leaders (persons whose power was evaluated similarly by both top leaders and other informants); (2) concealed leaders (persons assigned more power by top leaders than by other informants) and (3) symbolic leaders (persons assigned more power by other informants than by leaders). It was concluded that there are general relationships between visibility and power on the one hand and class and status on the other. Specifically, the author observes that: (1) visible leaders possess both power and high class and status rankings; (2) concealed leaders may possess power but have lower class or status ranking than visible leaders and (3) symbolic leaders possess high class and status ranking and this ranking, rather than their actual influence in community affairs, is a source of their reputation for power.

Bonjean, Charles M.; Browning, Harley L.; and Carter, Lewis F. "Toward Comparative Community Research: A Factor Analysis of United States Counties," *Sociological Quarterly* 10 (Spring 1969) 157-76.

This article is intended to provide assistance for scholars engaged in comparative research on community sociology by identifying the key features which differentiate communities. The authors expand upon Jonassen and Peres' study of Ohio counties (Christen J. Jonassen and Sherwood H. Peres, *Inter-relationships of Dimensions of Community Systems: A Factor Analysis of Eighty-two Variables* [Columbus: Ohio State University Press, 1960]) and Haddan and Borgatta's factor analysis of sixty-five variables operating in all American cities of 25,000 population or larger (Jeffery K. Hadden and Edgar F. Borgatta, *American Cities: Their Social Characteristics* [Chicago: Rand McNally & Company, 1965]). This investigation covers all counties in the forty-eight adjacent states and employs seventy-nine variables representative of all categories of data presented in the *County and City Data Book*. Of these, roughly two-thirds are the same or similar to the variables used in the earlier studies. The authors discuss eight factors explaining the greatest amount of variation (each more than 3.0 percent and total 56.7 percent) out of eighteen (explaining 78.6 percent of the total variation) extracted from the correlation matrix. The authors find agreement with both previous studies in that counties vary along dimensions which may be termed "Socioeconomic Status" (I–factor numbers ordered by amount of variance explained), "Residential Mobility" (IV), "Urbanism" (V), and (with less confidence) "Poverty" (XI). Along with the study of cities, it appears that communities vary along those dimensions mentioned above and dimensions called "Family Life Cycle" (II), "Manufacturing" (VI), and "Commercial Center" (VII) and (with less confidence) "Education Center" (X) and "Foreign Born Concentration" (XII). The only two factors found in this analysis but in neither of the other two studies were "Governmental Revenue and Expenditures" (III) and "Unemployment" (VIII).

Bonser, H.J.; Milk, R.G.; and Alred, C.E. *Local Leadership in Rural Communities of Kimberlin County, Tennessee,* Tennessee Agricultural Experiment Station, Agricultural Economy and Rural Sociology Department Monograph 144, December 1942.

Leaders of local neighborhood groups were interviewed to determine leadership characteristics. It was found that those with influence function chiefly on a person-to-person basis. While there was substantial similarity among leaders both in terms of traits and interests there was little cooperation between organizations. Leaders tended to function primarily within the confines of their neighborhood and special area of interest even though many held membership in more than one community service organization. Leaders as compared to nonleaders were older, better educated, better trained in their occupations, and valued conformity to local tradition as a most important leadership characteristic.

Booth, David A., and Adrian, Charles R. "Elections and Community Power," *Journal of Politics* 25 (February 1963) 107-18.

The locus for this study is a midwestern city dominated by large manufacturing which is traditionally Republican in its partisan politics. Local politics are nonpartisan but traditionally have been dominated by mainstreet businessmen or lawyers and by a group of financial and industrial leaders. The study focuses on the ease with which a relative newcomer to the community (a disc jockey) successfully challenged the established power structure and came to exercise substantial influence in community policies. The circumstances which allowed such access to an established power structure were: (1) change in the population composition; (2) access to the mass media by the new leader; (3) the new leader's exploitation of a specific issue during the city election and (4) an important schism within the traditional leadership structure which had been unprepared to deal with the challenge to its hegemony. The authors conclude that the sudden appearance of a new leader and the rather easy modification of the community power structure through election to the major political office in the city seem to lend support to those who have suggested that social scientists tend to overemphasize the solidity and stability of community power complexes.

Booth, David A., and Adrian, Charles R. "Power Structure and Community Change: A Replication Study of Community A," *Midwest Journal of Political Science* 6 (August 1962) 277-96.

This study replicates a 1954 study by Ralph Smuckler and George M. Belknap of a middle-sized Michigan community. Leaders were identified by a panel of persons "knowledgeable" in community affairs who were themselves nominated by a first-level panel of informants. Community decision making is seen as being dominated by two different groups who form "intersecting but non-concentric circles." Conflict between business and labor had increased. The distribution of influence in the community in 1961 is seen as somewhat more diffused than it was in 1954 and possible reasons for this diffusion are discussed.

Bouma, Donald H. "The Issue-Analysis Approach to Community Power: A Case Study of Realtors in Kalamazoo," *American Journal of Economics and Sociology* 29 (July 1970) 241-52.

This case study of an unsuccessful referendum on the creation of a housing commission seeks to assess certain aspects of social power in Kalamazoo. The objective was to assess the influence of various groups and organizations in the community decision-making process from the responses of interviews with a sample of 250 households. Although the proposal had been initially approved by the city council and had the support of almost every organization in the community, it was rejected because the real estate board was the key influential in the decision-making process. Six other explanations for the negative vote were found to be inadequate. The alleged influence of the realtors — the only opposition group — was based on the finding that voters rejected the proposal for the same reasons that realtors used in the campaign. The conclusion raises questions, in the author's opinion, about the validity of the reputational approach for determining social power because respondents did not identify the real estate board as an influential group in determining community decisions.

Bouma, Donald H. "Analysis of Social Power Position of a Real Estate Board," *Social Problems* 14 (Fall 1962) 121-32.

This study is an analysis of the basis for the dominant social power position of a real estate board in Grand Rapids, Michigan.

Bouma, Donald H. "The Legitimation of the Social Power Position of a Real Estate Board," *American Journal of Economics and Sociology* 21 (October 1962) 383-92.

Bradley, Donald S., and Zald, Mayer L. "From Commercial to Political Administration Recruitment of the Mayors of Chicago," *American Journal of Sociology* 71 (September 1965) 153-67.

The social and economic background of the thirty-nine mayors of Chicago who held office from 1837 to 1965 is examined. On the basis of this evidence it is concluded that the community has undergone shifts in the distribution of political influence over that period of time and that influence which once rested with economic and social dominants now rests with the Democratic party.

Burgess, M. Elaine. *Negro Leadership in a Southern City* (Chapel Hill: University of North Carolina Press, 1962).

Reviews:

Wilson, James Q. *American Journal of Sociology* 68 (September 1962) 268-69.

Sutton, Willis A., Jr. *Social Forces* 41 (October 1962) 96.

The site of this study is a middle-sized southern city where there is a sizable Negro upper class with a strong economic base. The city is the home of three institutions of higher learning and the white leadership is described as moderate.

Negro leadership is identified in each of four ways: (1) twenty-eight persons were nominated by a panel of "knowledgeables" in the Negro community and these nominees were then asked to rate each other's influence; (2) actual participation in the five major decisions facing the Negro community during the three-year study period was determined; (3) twenty white leaders (selected by the reputational approach) were asked to nominate and rank Negro influentials; and (4) a sample of 283 Negro residents was asked to identify leaders.

The findings of all four measures were correlated highly. While there was some specialization of leadership for specific issues, the leaders were generally influential across a number of issues of different content. Community action was funneled through a single Negro organization and this organization – the "Crescent Negro Council" – provided a unified center of power in the community. Perhaps as a result of this unity of leadership, the Negro community is seen as politically effective in the larger community.

Carney, Francis M. "The Decentralized Politics of Los Angeles," *Annals of the American Academy of Political and Social Science* 353 (May 1964) 107-21.

The author concludes that public policy decisions in Los Angeles are made largely by the constitutionally designated public officials responsible for various policy jurisdictions and that "there is no power elite in any meaningful sense of the word." Power in Los Angeles is seen as widely diffused in both the political and social realms. Some of the factors which contribute to this diffusion are: (1) nonpartisan district elections for the 15-member city council; (2) the weak constitutional position of the mayor's office; (3) the tremendous influx of population and the high mobility of city residents within the metropolitan area; (4) the low sense of civic identification on the part of citizens, as well as social and economic elites; (5) the substantial diversity within the population and the absence of any structural mechanisms for integration; and (6) the low salience of politics to many of the residents of the region.

Clark, Terry N. "Community Structure, Decision Making, Budget Expenditures, and Urban Renewal in 51 American Communities," in Charles M. Bonjean, Terry N. Clark and Robert L. Lineberry, eds., *Community Politics: A Behavioral Approach* (New York: The Free Press, 1971). Revised and expanded from a paper with the same title published in the *American Sociological Review* 33 (August 1968) 576-93.

Moving beyond the question "who governs?", the author explores not only the causes of a community's influence structure but its consequences on outputs as well in a large number of communities. This study is based on fifty-one cities for which statistical data about community characteristics was gathered as well as interview data with eleven strategically placed informants in each community. They were questioned about four particular issues which tend to involve different types of community actors in differing relations with one another – urban renewal, mayoral election, air pollution and the anti-poverty program. The community decision-making structure was measured by using "the ersatz decisional method." Features examined were the number of major actors involved in each issue area and the degree to which decision-makers overlapped from one issue area to the next, from which an index of decentralization was constructed based on the assumption that the greater the number of participants and the less overlap, the greater the decentralization or pluralism in the system. The interrelationships among city characteristics, decision-making structure and policy outputs were specified by use of multiple regression analysis. Central findings were: (1) as predicted, decentralized decision making was positively associated with economic diversification and population size, and negatively associated with reformed governmental institutions;

(2) decentralization of decision making was positively associated with both budget expenditures and urban renewal expenditures, which contradicted the author's hypotheses regarding outputs.

Clark, Terry N., ed. *Comparative Research on Community Decision Making,* special issue of *The New Atlantis* 1, No. 2 (Winter 1970).

The articles presented in this issue grew out of concern with the extent to which earlier research in the United States on community power and decision making may be extended to other countries — especially European countries. In general the contributors have been concerned with two questions: first, what lessons may be drawn from the mistakes as well as the accomplishments of research undertaken in the United States in order to better understand another country?; and, second, to what degree will patterns of community power and decision making identified in the United States take on greater perspective through comparison with patterns in other countries? The authors and titles included in the issue are the following:

Clark, "Introduction to the Issue: Current Topics in Research on Community Decision Making."

William Kornblum, "The Yugloslav Communal System: Decision Making in Housing and Urban Development."

Janez Jerovšek, "The Structure of Influence in the Yugoslav Commune."

Mark Kesselman, "Research Choices in Comparative Local Politics."

Charles Roig, Christian Mingasson, and Pierre Kukawka, "Social Structure and Local Power Structure in Urban Areas, Analysis of 17 French Townships."

Michael Aiken and Robert R. Alford, "Comparative Urban Research and Community Decision Making."

D. S. Morris and K. Newton, "Profile of a Local Political Elite: Businessmen as Community Decision Makers in Birmingham, 1838-1966."

Jörgen Westerstahl, "The Communal Research Program in Sweden."

Peter Friedmann, "Community Decision Making in the United States: A Review of Recent Research."

Clelland, Donald A., and Form, William H. "Economic Dominants and Community Power: A Comparative Analysis," *American Journal of Sociology* 69 (March 1964) 511-21.

This study is a replication and extension of research undertaken in "Cibola" (Ypsilanti, Michigan) by Robert Schulze. The authors seek to test Schulze's hypothesis that economic elites tend to disassociate themselves from local politics when the company they manage is absentee-owned or integrated into national markets. In the community studied by the authors, which they call "Wheelsburg" (Lansing, Michigan) the authors identify political and civic leaders in terms of: (1) positions held by economic dominants over an extended period of time in political and civic activities; (2) the current reputation for leadership possessed by economic dominants and (3) the role that current economic dominants play in specific community issues and programs.

It is concluded that Schulze's hypothesis is generally valid but that different conditions in the two cities are associated with a slower rate of withdrawal on the part of community dominants from political and civic affairs in Wheelsburg. Among the relevant variables which differentiate the two communities is the absence of local party politics and the lack of ethnic and class cleavage in Wheelsburg as compared to Cibola.

Cowgill, Donald O. "Power as Process in an Urban Community," in Richard Stauber, ed., *Approaches to the Study of Urbanization,* (Lawrence, Kansas: Governmental Research Center Series, 27, 1964) pp. 168-75.

On the basis of his study of participation in six key decisions in Wichita, Kansas, the author concludes that power in Wichita should be conceived as a "fluid process." He rejects the notion that Wichita is ruled by either a monolithic elite or a polynucleated or multi-factional structure; "Instead, we see various interest groups bestirring themselves when their interests are affected and not participating in decision making when their interests are not affected." He considers the possibility of measuring "potential power" and rejects it as unrealistic.

Dahl, Robert A. *Who Governs? Democracy and Power in an American City* (New Haven: Yale University Press, 1961).

Reviews:

Knepper, David W., *Journal of Politics* 24 (August 1962) 620-22.

Rogers, David, *American Journal of Sociology* 68 (September 1962) 271-72.

Price, Hugh Douglas, *Yale Law Journal* 71 (July 1962) 1589-96.

Hunter, Floyd, *Administrative Science Quarterly* 6 (March 1962) 517-19.

Goldstein, Marshall N., *American Sociological Review* 27 (December 1962) 860-62.

Price, Hugh Douglas, *Political Science Quarterly* 77 (June 1962) 269-71.

Eulau, Heinz, *American Political Science Review* 56 (March 1962) 144-45.

Padover, Saul K., *Social Research* 29 (Winter 1962) 489-94.

Holland, Henry M., Jr., *Social Forces* 41 (March 1963) 322-23.

Janowitz, Morris, *Public Opinion Quarterly* 26 (Fall 1962) 398-410.

In his study of New Haven, Connecticut (population 150,000), the author observes that historically economic and social dominants have played a decreasingly important role as holders of formal positions of influence in the community. Then, based on his study of the actual decision-making process in three key areas (urban redevelopment, education and nominations for political office) as well as interviews with key participants in the decision-making process and a random sample of the voters in New Haven, Dahl concludes that power is broadly diffused and shared in New Haven. With the exception of the mayor and his immediate associates, influence of individuals in community decisions tends to be limited to one general area of concern. A typology of community power structures is developed. Dahl describes the dynamics of the political process in great detail and constructs, on the basis of his findings, a general theory of democratic politics.

Dakin, Ralph E. "Variations in Power Structures and Organizing Efficiency: A Comparative Study of Four Areas," *Sociological Quarterly* 3 (July 1962) 228-50.

The author looks at four quasi-rural areas ranging in size from 2,700 to 14,200 residents and from 20 square miles to 320 square miles in area. These communities were chosen because they differed widely in their capacity to organize watershed districts under federal and state legislation. Persons who were generally influential in each area were identified by "knowledgeables." The number of influentials varied from 40 to 50 in each case.

Influentials in the areas which were more efficient in organizing for action on the one issue studied differed from influentials in less efficient areas in the following ways: (1) they were better educated; (2) they had higher status occupations generally associated with organizational skills and experience;(3) they were more integrated socially; (4) they were more active in civic associations;(5) they participated to a greater degree in the development of the watershed district.

Note: Another report on this study which discusses its implications for public policy appeared under the title, "Social Variables and Organizing Efficiency: A Method," in Richard L. Stauber, ed., *Approaches to the Study of Urbanization* (Lawrence, Kansas: Governmental Research Series, 27, 1964) pp. 156-67.

Daland, Robert T. *Dixie City: A Portrait of Political Leadership* (University of Alabama Bureau of Public Administration, 1956).

This study of a rapidly growing city in Alabama (population 50,000), focuses on access to, and possession of, positions of formal leadership, (i.e., elected political office). Forty-seven persons were interviewed including all available elected officeholders (commissioners) or their closest living relatives. The author finds that competition for political office was sporadic; less than half of the elections were contested and incumbents tended to be reelected. Successful candidates were professionals or businessmen, i.e., lawyers, merchants, real estate or insurance men, and most were born inside the county and lived in a relatively well defined "better section" in the older part of town. No Negroes sought political office in Dixie City, although Negroes comprised 25 percent of the city's residents. Increasing urbanization seemed to lessen the importance of native origin as a political asset and also increased the costs of running for public office and the time required to serve as an elected official, thus opening access to positions of influence.

D'Antonio, William V., and Form, William H. *Influentials in Two Border Cities: A Study in Community Decision-Making* (Notre Dame, Indiana: University of Notre Dame Press, 1965).

Reviews:
   Walton, John, *American Journal of Sociology* 71 (May 1966) 725-26.
   Mott, Paul E., *Annals* 367 (September 1966) 213-15.
   Young, Ruth, *American Sociological Review* 31 (August 1966) 556-57.
   Rose, Arnold M., *Sociology Quarterly* 7 (Fall 1966) 517-18.
   Burgess, M. Elaine, *Social Forces* 44 (June 1966) 606-07.
   Kemper, Tiffany, *Sociology and Social Research* 51 (October 1966) 127-28.
Community leaders in El Paso, Texas, and Ciudad Juarez, Mexico, were identified in 1955 by a number of "knowledgeables" from the business and

governmental sectors in each community. "Knowledgeables" were most likely to nominate people in their own sector as influential.

Government officials were considered much more influential in community affairs in Ciudad Juarez than in El Paso. The power of government officials in El Paso was limited to the area of their formal authority, whereas businessmen tended to be generally influential. The authors examine and compare the existing integration and cleavage among influentials in both cities. (See the comment on the article authored by Form and D'Antonio entitled, "Integration and Cleavage Among Community Influentials in Two Border Cities.")

In 1958, the authors replicated their earlier efforts to identify influentials. About 45 percent of those influential in 1955 were not influential in 1958 in Ciudad Juarez. In El Paso there was a 40 percent turnover in influentials. The status of politicians was more vulnerable than businessmen in both cities and the top-ranked persons in 1955 were more likely than lower ranked persons to maintain status.

In both cities, businessmen were more likely than government-affiliated persons to be selected as most influential in a hypothetical hospital project.

However, it is concluded that business does not dominate either city. "Loose overlapping coalitions of business and political groups seemed to characterize El Paso, while three [party] factions . . . , plus some neutrals and independents, dominated the Ciudad Juarez scene." (Including some federal officials.)

Four major issues over eight years were studied in El Paso and seven issues in eight years were studied in Ciudad Juarez. No more than 40 percent of the reputed influentials in either city participated in *one* or more decisions. Reputation was a better predictor of actual involvement for political influentials than for business influentials. Top-rated influentials were more likely to be actually involved than other influentials.

D'Antonio, William V.; Form, William H.; Loomis, Charles P.; and Erickson, Eugene C. "Institutional and Occupational Representations in Eleven Community Influence Systems," *American Sociological Review* 26 (June 1961) 440-46.

Community leaders in six southwestern American communities, two Mexican communities, a northwestern community (Seattle, Washington), a southeastern city (Atlanta, Georgia), and an English city (Bristol), are identified by panels of "knowledgeables" in each city. Ten institutional sectors are identified. The sectors represented among the influentials varied from five in San Diego to ten in Denver.

As compared to all other occupational types, businessmen made up a greater proportion of community leaders in all of the communities – especially in the American cities. The highest representation from the governmental sector among the leaders in these communities was found in the Mexican and English cities. "Key influentials" were distinguished from other influentials (according to the frequency with which they were nominated as leaders) and it is concluded that the background of these persons is similar (in most cities) to the background of influentials. It is hypothesized that community size is not related to the degree of dominance of the community by businessmen.

Dye, Thomas. "Popular Images of Decision Making in Suburban Communities," *Sociology and Social Research* 47 (October 1962) 75-83.

Eagleton Institute of Politics, Rutgers University. *Urban Leadership in Latin America* (Report to the United States Agency for International Development, 1964).

Edwards, Harold T. "Power Structure and its Communication Behavior in San Jose, Costa Rica," *Journal of Inter-American Studies* 10 (April 1967) 236-47.

The purpose of the San Jose study was to employ the reputational method in a cross-cultural situation using a broader scope to measure reputed power, in order to strengthen it as a research tool and to provide more objective data for future comparison. The main departure from earlier studies was to use a composite rank score for each influential based on four different questions: (1) an open-ended question asking the twenty-nine top leaders (identified by a panel) to name the five most influential people in the community; (2) a perception rank scale of the other twenty-eight top leaders; and (3) two questions in which the top leaders were asked to name the four people who would be most capable of establishing a new orphanage and initiating a new industry. To determine the inter-group communication of influentials, each was asked to check the frequency of communication — in formal settings, informal settings, and in written form — with the other influentials. The procedure employed identified an influential group, and furthermore, the information on communication patterns established that it is a functioning power complex. Two clusters of leaders identified with different political parties and different occupational interests were delineated as well as the key individual who provided liaison between the two clusters. The findings show that the reputational technique is useful as a tool for determining community influence in a cross-cultural situation, and that the technique can be adapted to objectively locate sub-groups or cliques.

Fanelli, A. Alexander. "A Typology of Community Leadership Based on Influence and Interaction Within the Leader Sub-System," *Social Forces* 34 (May 1956) 332-38.

In this study of "Bakerville," Mississippi (population 5,000) a sample of 304 white adults was asked to identify community leaders. Of the twenty-five persons nominated as leaders, thirteen were businessmen, seven were government officials and five were professionals. Twenty of the leaders themselves were then asked to nominate those among them with whom they would wish to work on three types of community projects and also to specify the nature of their interaction with other leaders. With the exception of the newspaper editor, none of the leaders were influential in several problem areas. The author concludes, therefore, that leadership in Bakerville is specialized. Using the leaders' own rankings of influence and matching these with the patterns of communication among the leaders, the author develops a fourfold typology of community leadership. These types are: (1) "active influentials" who are seen by both citizens and other leaders as influential and who discuss problems with most other leaders; (2) leaders who are highly regarded by the general population, called "prestige leaders," who belong to fewer organizations and were less likely to communicate with other leaders than the "active influentials;" (3) "active subinfluentials" who are seen by few other leaders as powerful and (4) "lesser leaders."

Negroes, who comprise 40 percent of the population of Bakerville, were excluded from the study.

Faunce, William A., and Clelland, Donald A. "Professionalization and Stratification Patterns in an Industrial Community," *American Journal of Sociology* 72 (January 1967) 341-50.

The findings of this study are based on an analysis of a Michigan community of 25,000 inhabitants where half of the labor force is employed by one large company. Three hundred and twenty-seven persons from various occupations were interviewed concerning their attitudes toward the community, their participation in community activities, and their perceptions of class, status, and power arrangements.

On the basis of their data, the authors argue that new patterns of industrialization will increase the percentage of professionals and technicians in the labor force and that these persons, unlike managers, owners, and other economic elites, tend to be active in community affairs. They have high attributed power and they perceive themselves as powerful. They also hold increasing amounts of power. The authors observe that professionals tend to identify with middle-class values rather than upper class. They argue that other communities will reach a similar stage of industrialization to that of the studied community and may therefore experience similar community involvement by professionals and technicians. They conclude that "class status and power arrangements are, in large part, a function of the organizational structure, production technology, and form of division of labor in industrial communities."

Form, William H. "Organized Labor's Place in the Community Power Structure," *Industrial and Labor Relations Review* 12 (July 1959) 526-39.

Forty top leaders in Lansing, Michigan (population 100,000) were identified by a panel of fourteen "knowledgeables" who represented seven institutional sectors. Only two of these top influentials were labor officials. Moreover, labor's activity in the community's nonpartisan elections seemed to be relatively inconsequential. Only 15 percent of the persons who held positions on formal governmental bodies (city boards and commissions) were working class. Even fewer union members were elected to the Board of Education. Participation and attributed influence of labor officials and union members were low in all areas of community activities, even the activities of the Democratic party. Among various sectors of community life the strength of labor influence varied from highest in economic bargaining and became decreasingly less significant in areas of welfare, education, political parties, elective municipal offices, city appointive boards, religion, and mass communications, where it was virtually nonexistent. It is concluded that organized labor's influence in the community power structure lags well behind its influence in economic matters in the industries with which it is involved.

Form, William H., and D'Antonio, William V. "Integration and Cleavage Among Community Influentials in Two Border Cities,"*American Sociological Review* 24 (December 1959) 804-14.

Leaders in El Paso, Texas and Ciudad Juarez, Mexico are identified by a panel of nominators in each city. American business and political influentials tended to be more integrated than the Mexican leaders in four ways: (1) in El Paso leaders were more likely to be seen as influentials in both political and business spheres; (2) there was less differentiation in the social profiles of business and political influentials in El Paso; (3) agreement on their perceptions of institutional practices and relations in both the economic and political spheres was more pronounced among the influentials in Ciudad Juarez and (4) there was greater consensus among business and political influentials in El Paso concerning the nature of the major local issues.

In neither city is the power system seen as a monolithic hierarchy. It is hypothesized that community conflict in the United States is not institutionally based but takes place among differing coalitions of business and political influentials. In Mexico, on the other hand, conflict is more likely to take place between economic and political institutions.

Form, William H., and Miller, Delbert C. *Industry, Labor and Community* (New York: Harper and Brothers, 1960).

Reviews:

    McConnell, John W., *American Sociological Review* 26 (February 1961) 132-33.

    Schneider, Eugene V., *American Journal of Sociology* 68 (May 1963) 700-01.

    Knox, John B., *Social Forces* 39 (March 1961) 275-76.

This study explores the relationship between industry and labor on the one hand, and various community institutions on the other. Special emphasis is placed on the role of industry and labor in influencing social and political policies in a number of different communities in the United States, Mexico and England. It is concluded that labor invariably plays a minor role in community affairs while most communities, at least in the United States, are dominated by their business elites — whether the economic base of these elites is home grown or not.

Form, William H., and Sauer, Warren L. *Community Influentials in a Middle-Sized City: A Case Study* (East Lansing: Institute for Community Development, Michigan State University, 1960).

A panel of fourteen "knowledgeables" from seven major areas of community life identified a list of 120 influentials in Lansing, Michigan (population 100,000). Of these, the forty most frequently nominated were interviewed. Four-fifths of these were businessmen. These economic dominants tended to avoid active participation in party or municipal politics but were quite active in business and civic activities in the community. It was widely assumed by these influentials that businessmen and business organizations were the most powerful in the community.

Economic dominants belonged, on the average, to thirteen organizations. They saw themselves as responsible and as acting in the best interests of the community. As a group, they expressed little concern over such problems as full employment, race relations, adequate housing or better education. While there was substantial value consensus among these influentials, they acknowledged that they did not always agree and that they did not always act concerning those matters on which they did reach consensus.

Fowler, Irving A. "Local Industrial Structure, Economic Power and Community Welfare," *Social Problems* 6 (Summer 1958) 41-51.

Based on a study of thirty New York cities, ranging in population from 10,000 to 80,000, the author seeks to establish the relationship between the distribution of economic power among economic institutions, the nature of the local power structure, and each city's ranking on a social welfare index. The index involved forty-eight variables measuring personal income and security, housing, health, education, political participation, and municipal wealth and services.

The author concludes that: (1) small-business cities had somewhat lower levels of welfare than big-business cities (contrary to findings by Mills and Ulmer); (2) type of industry was related to welfare — heavy industry and concentrated employment was positively associated with higher social welfare; (3) least pluralistic power structures (defined as those with concentrated employment, low industrial unionism, a small "old" middle class, low political "liberalism," and low population heterogeneity) were associated with higher welfare levels.

Freeman, Charles, and Mayo, Selz C. "Decision Makers in Rural Community Action," *Social Forces* 35 (May 1957) 319-22.

Leaders of "Union," North Carolina (population 925) were identified by three independent measures: (a) participation in organization; (b) nomination by a panel of "knowledgeables" and (c) participation in one or more of forty-one community decisions over a two-year period. There was a general positive relationship between an individual's standing on the three measures. Those with highest leadership rankings interacted most with other leaders and tended to make both major and minor decisions.

The authors do not explicitly deal with the number of persons at each level of the leadership structure or the socioeconomic characteristics of leaders.

Freeman, Linton C.; Bloomberg, Warner, Jr.; Koff, Stephen P.; Sunshine, Morris H.; and Fararo, Thomas J. *Local Community Leadership* (Syracuse, N.Y.: Syracuse University, University College Paper No. 15, 1960).

In this study dealing with the resolution of community problems in Syracuse, New York (population 345,000) the authors systematically identified thirty-nine important community-wide issues which were acted upon between 1955 and 1960. More than 600 interviews were held with persons who were alleged to have participated in the resolution of these issues or who held formal positions of responsibility with regard to these issues. In addition, a sample survey of 215 community residents was carried out.

Clusters of leadership were identified and it was determined that less than three-tenths of one percent of the adult citizens participated in a direct way in decision making (in any of the thirty-nine issues studied). Influence was widely disbursed within this elite group and leadership groups tended to focus on relatively narrow problem areas. There was no general power elite found in Syracuse, although, with the exception of a few labor leaders, most decision-makers came from relatively high socioeconomic backgrounds. However, there was an overall trend suggesting the diminution of influence based on social prestige or wealth alone and an increase in the influence of technical specialists.

Freeman, Linton, C. *Patterns of Local Community Leadership* (Indianapolis: Bobbs-Merrill, 1968).

Reviews:
Corwin, R. David, *American Journal of Sociology* 74 (May 1969) 743-44.
Hanson, David J., *American Journal of Sociology* 74 (May 1969) 743-44.
Leadley, Samuel M., *Rural Sociology* 34 (March 1969).

This book reports on a three-year study of the leadership and decision-making structure of Syracuse, New York. The author attempts to answer three critical questions in the study of community power: What is a community leader? To what degree is leadership concentrated? What factors affect differential rates of leadership by different segments of the population?

Freeman finds that the methods used in the research shape the picture of the decision-making process, but he concludes that power in Syracuse is relatively diffused and issue-defined. It is suggested that as Syracuse became more complex socially and economically power became more decentralized and that some of the conflicting findings of other students of community power may be traced to the fact that the places studied were in different phases of urbanization and industrialization.

French, Robert Mills. "Change Comes to Cornucopia — Industry and the Community," in Robert Mills French, ed., *The Community: A Comparative Perspective* (Itasca, Illinois: F.E. Peacock Publishers, Inc., 1969).

In the town of Cornucopia, Illinois (population about 11,000) the author has studied the transition of the community power structure with changing characteristics of the local economy. In 1964, one year before a large assembly plant employing 5,000 workers was to open, and in 1967, after it had been in operation for two years, the structure of community power was assessed by employing the reputational, positional and decision-making techniques. In addition, an early period when the town's economy was dominated by a single locally-owned firm was reconstructed through records, old newspapers, and interviews with survivors.

The author concludes that control of the economy has been the key element in the transition of the community power structure. In the early period the locally-owned and managed industry was able to wield pyramidal control. When the firm closed down in 1952, local factions moved in to claim the power once held by industrialists, but none was able to wield absolute power and factionalism characterized the power structure. The impact of the new absentee-owned firm which dominated the local economy was to introduce signs of pluralism into the system. Bifurcation — which occurs when nationally-linked corporations with wide-ranging interests replace local industry — results in a division of power between local leaders, whose dominant concerns become community projects, and the absentee-owner which controls the community's economic dealings. When the community realized its dependence on the absentee-owned corporation and its freedom from local figures, the local social-political sphere became more pluralistic, because of the limits imposed on the control of local leaders over all spheres of life and because the local dominant group appeared assailable. The author thus describes this power structure as bifurcated pluralism.

French, Robert Mills, ed. *The Community: A Comparative Perspective* (Itasca, Illinois: F.E. Peacock Publishers, Inc., 1969).

Frykenberg, Robert Eric. "Traditional Processes of Power in South India: An Historical Analysis of Local Influence," in Reinhard Bendix, ed., *State and Society: A Reader in Comparative Political Sociology* (Boston: Little, Brown and Company, 1968) pp. 107-125.

The author surveys the history of the Guntar District in South India in terms of the interaction between centralized powers and the localizing tendencies of village elites. Under successive empires from medieval times through the British India Company, local elite groups and institutions were able to survive the intrusions of exogenous forces. Outside rule, based on administrative control for the collection of taxes, depended on indigenous scribes and the rare knowledge of clerical skills was monopolized by families and castes who systematically worked to undermine central control. The theoretical focus of this article is locality in conflict with the larger system, and the author develops the concept of "anti-state" to refer to the kind of political system "which, residing in a state, disperses its power and proliferates itself to the detriment of the state and acts in such a way that it not only naturally opposes but actually prevents the state from functioning properly."

Gamberg, Herbert. *The Escape from Power: Politics in the American Community,* Exchange Bibliography No. 106 (Monticello, Ill.: Council of Planning Librarians, November, 1969).

In this study of Peoria, Illinois (population 103,162) with some consideration of Rockford, and Springfield, Illinois, the author seeks to delineate the power structure in these towns and to set forth an approach to the study of community power which overcomes the weaknesses of earlier approaches, represented by Hunter and Dahl. The author finds shortcomings in the former, and basic theoretical deficiencies in the pluralism approach, specifically its individualization of power, its accent on concrete issues as the exclusive focus of power, and its "essentially economic model of power."

The author proceeds to analyze three issues which have arisen in Peoria — governmental reorganization, annexation, and open occupancy in public housing — by investigating the structure of power through "repute sociometry" and the structure of the process of decision making. The major conclusions are: (1) an "organized plutocracy" appears on occasion but is not enduring; (2) even when a "Hunter pyramid" exists, the impetus of its organization and the source of its innovative ideas often come from a small body of professionals and middle-class activists; (3) power is, however, not spread among individuals throughout the community, and prestige, legitimate wealth and executive occupation assure position at the top of the community power pyramid; and (4) the reluctance of the powerful to lead often creates a power vacuum which can be filled by men of perhaps less formal power. Examination of the issues corroborates, in the author's opinion, the utility of his conception of power, summarized as follows: "power is structured in institutions rather than persons, involves maintenance and control as well as change and decision making, must be studied in historical depth to be fully understood, and is legitimated by commonly accepted value systems."

Gans, Herbert J. *The Levittowners: Ways of Life and Politics in a New Suburban Community* (New York: Pantheon Books, 1967).

This very thorough study of the early development of Levittown, New Jersey (now renamed Willingboro) uses various study methods including mailed questionnaires, interviews and participant observation to examine ways in which the cultural and social life of the community shape the nature of politics in the decision-making process. Gans concludes that while the power structure in the community may be somewhat more monolithic than those found by political scientists in established communities, citizens enjoy considerable access in relative terms to the decision-making process and the absence of a socioeconomic underclass contributes to minimizing the extent to which any group or type of citizen is excluded. The power structure, he suggests, is comprised of incumbent party leaders, elected officials, the community developer and his organization and "the Catholic bloc." With the exception of the builder, those with greatest influence tend to be leading citizens, politicians, and municipal officials rather than business leaders, although this was in part related to the relative absence of commercial and industrial interests found in more diversified communities.

Goodall, Leonard, ed. *Urban Politics in the Southwest* (Tempe: Arizona State University, Institute of Public Administration, 1967).

This volume collects eleven studies of cities in the southwestern United States. The studies, organized in similar formats, are focused on formal governmental processes. In general, the studies conclude that political decision making is dominated by white collar elites and that the intensity of political activity, especially with respect to the nonpartisan elections in these cities, is usually quite low. Labor unions and ethnic groups play varying but minimally effective roles in influencing city policies. Contributors to the book and the cities they studied are: Dorothy I. Cline and T. Phillip Wolf, Albuquerque; David M. Olson, Austin; August O. Spain, Fort Worth; Clifton McCleskey, Houston; George J. Mauer, Oklahoma City; Leonard E. Goodall, Phoenix; Bill Crane, San Antonio; Robert F. Wilcox, San Diego; Conrad Joyner, Tucson; Bertil Hanson, Tulsa; Dwight M. Carpenter, Wichita; and Robert W. Glasgow, the Southwest.

Hanna, William John, in collaboration with Hanna, Judith Lynne. "Influence and Influentials in Two Urban-Centered African Communities," *Comparative Politics* 2 (October 1969) 17-40.

Political influence in two small urban-centered African communities — Umuahia in Eastern Nigeria and Mbale, Uganda, both about 28,000 in population in 1967 — was studied comparatively, using equivalent techniques. A panel of eighteen knowledgeables was selected in each city composed of nine government officials and nine from other sectors of the community. (Government was highly represented because of the presumed high relative importance of government and the underdevelopment of some institutional sectors in local African communities.) Influentials identified by the panel were interviewed, and, in addition, a small probability sample of adults on voter rolls was selected and interviewed. An important difference in the political cultures of the two communities was the far lower communality of perspectives on who has influence in the ethnically heterogeneous Ugandan community in comparison to the Ibo-dominated Nigerian community. Having assessed the bases of influence, the authors conclude that it is based on "attainment" – that is, within a circle limited by ascriptive criteria, recruitment to positions of influence is based on achievement.

Hawley, Amos H. "Community Power and Urban Renewal Success," *American Journal of Sociology* 68 (June 1963) 422-31.

Starting from the premise that power is an attribute of a social system rather than of an individual, this study examines the relationship between the extent of power concentration and urban renewal success. Concentration of power is defined in terms of the proportion of managers, proprietors and officials in the total labor force in the 194 cities with a population of over 50,000 which are used in the study. The author finds a statistically significant relationship between the high concentration of power (a low ratio of managers, proprietors and officials in the total labor force) and success in implementing urban renewal programs. This relationship holds up under a series of control conditions.

Hay, Donald G., and Ensminger, Douglas. "Leader-Follower Patterns in Selected Maine Towns," *Rural Sociology* 14 (June 1949) 160-63.

Hicks, Frederic. "Politics, Power, and the Role of the Village Priest in Paraguay," *Journal of Inter-American Studies* 9 (April 1967) 273-82.

This study seeks to explain the extraordinary amount of power and influence which priests in small Paraguayan towns are reputed to possess. Since the church is weaker in Paraguay than in many other Latin American countries, their influence cannot be viewed as simply an extension of the power of the church. The study took place in the town of Capiata (population 2,000) located in a *distrito* of 25,000 people, which is the unit to which the priest is responsible. The political culture in Paraguay is such that all people are identified publicly with one of the two major parties or one of its factions; unswerving partisanship is a political norm, with the exception that priests are considered neutral. "In this situation, a prominent individual who is politically neutral is needed in the community to serve as an intermediary in a variety of situations." This individual need not necessarily be the priest, but if there is a priest in town "he is the one most likely to have the necessary qualifications." While the priest may not accept this role, there are pressures on him to do so, and if accepted the priest is likely to become a very influential and powerful person.

Holden, David. "La Estructura del Liderazgo y sus Caracteristicas en una Comunidad de Costa Rica," *Journal of Inter-American Economic Studies* 70 (January 1966) 129-41.

Hollingshead, August E. *Elmstown's Youth* (New York: John Wiley and Sons, Inc., 1949).

In this study of Morris, Illinois, the author utilizes the anthropological approach to the study of community and focuses on the nature of the social stratification in the community. He concludes that power is concentrated in the hands of the upper class and that upper-class persons dominate both political parties, as well as a number of other community institutions. These social and economic dominants are seen as relatively cohesive in terms of values and objectives.

Hoskin, Gary. "Power Structure in a Venezuelan Town: The Case of San Cristobal," *International Journal of Comparative Sociology* 9 (September-December 1968) 188-207.

In this study of a city in southwestern Venezuela (population 122,000 in 1965), the author employed both the reputational approach and the analysis of key issues. In the reputational analysis, forty-three leaders were selected for interviews from the ratings by seven judges of names submitted by leaders of thirteen sectors of community life. The two approaches provide complementary evidence; the author finds that policy making tends to be controlled by a few individuals of recognized power, "but because the leaders at the apex of the power structure are not located within the same power clusters and do not share common attitudes and policy orientations, no single, cohesive elite dominates the community." Community power is, however, highly transitory because of (1) realignments taking place within the power structure as ascriptive, upper-class leaders are losing influence to modernizing politics and functionally based leaders, and (2) the high association between influence and key positions in government and political parties, which are subject to rapid turnover.

Hunter, Floyd. *Community Power Structure* (Chapel Hill: University of North Carolina Press, 1953).

Reviews:
London, Jack, *American Journal of Sociology* 60 (March 1955) 522-23.
Strong, Donald S., *American Political Science Review* 48 (March 1954) 235-37.
Smith, Louis, *Journal of Politics* 16 (February 1954) 146-50.
Mills, C. Wright, *Social Forces* 32 (October 1953) 92-93.
Dahl, Robert A., *Journal of Politics* 22 (February 1960) 148-51.
Kaufman, Herbert and Jones, Victor, "The Mystery of Power," *Public Administration Review* 14 (Summer 1954) 205-12.

Those who hold power in "Regional City" (Atlanta, Georgia) (population about 300,000 in 1951) are identified by a panel of knowledgeable "judges." The forty most often nominated as influentials were then made the object of study and investigation and twenty-seven of these influentials were interviewed. The interaction among these leaders was mapped sociometrically and conclusions were drawn as to who influenced whom within the leadership structure. The author concludes that Regional City was controlled by a small, relatively cohesive economic elite whose influence in community affairs was, for the most part, not visible to the city population.

Hunter, Floyd; Schaffer, Ruth Conner; and Sheps, Cecil G. *Community Organization: Action and Inaction* (Chapel Hill: University of North Carolina Press, 1956).

Using the reputational technique of identifying community influentials, the authors conclude that the decision-making process in Salem, Massachusetts, (population about 3,000 in 1950) is dominated by local businessmen.

Izmirlian, H., Jr. "The Implications of Political Structure for Economic Behavior: A Study in the Communication of Ideas," *Asian Survey* 8 (November 1968) 911-20.

The political structures of two Indian (Punjabi) villages are found to evolve from being self-contained and traditional to being more fluid and linked with the leadership in larger political units. These changes were brought about by, and interacted with, the breakdown of traditional economic patterns and the changes in values and communication patterns associated with economic changes.

Janowitz, Morris, ed. *Community Political Systems* (Glencoe, Illinois: The Free Press, 1961).

Reviews:

Vidich, A., *Annals* 338 (November 1961) 144-45.

Vines, Kenneth N., *Journal of Politics* 24 (February 1962) 204-06.

Wingfield, Clyde J., "Attitudes and Action: The Politics of Influence," *Public Administration Review* 22 (Winter 1962) 41-45.

Miller, Delbert C., *American Journal of Sociology* 67 (September 1961) 215.

Notestein, Robert B., *Sociology Quarterly* 2 (October 1961) 310-12.

Jennings, M. Kent, *Social Forces* 40 (March 1962) 273-74.

This collection of essays, all of which are based on field studies, deal with a number of aspects of community life both in the United States and abroad. The material herein was prepared especially for this volume and the articles by Robert Shulze and Harry Scoble deal most directly with the question of the distribution of influence in American communities. (For a summary of these articles, consult the authors' names.)

Jennings, M. Kent. *Community Influentials: The Elites of Atlanta* (Glencoe, Illinois: The Free Press, 1964).

Reviews:

Milbrath, Lester W., *Journal of Politics* 27 (May 1965) 437-38.

Miller, Delbert C., *Administrative Science Quarterly* 9 (March 1965) 443-45.

Rossi, Peter H., *American Journal of Sociology* 71 (May 1966) 723-25.

Kellstadt, Lyman, "Atlanta to Oretown: Identifying Community Elites," *Public Administration Review* 25 (June 1965) 161-68.

D'Antonio, William V., *American Sociological Review* 30 (June 1965) 455-56.

Hill, Richard J., *Social Forces* 43 (March 1965) 440-41.

The community leadership of Atlanta, Georgia (Floyd Hunter's "Regional City,") is identified by three methods: (1) leaders are nominated by a panel of knowledgeable "judges" (the author calls these "attributed" leaders); (2) by the position they hold in public office ("prescribed leaders") and (3) by possession of wealth and/or a position of influence in major economic institutions (these are described as "economic dominants"). The role of each of these groups in the determination of major issues is studied and it is concluded that leadership of Atlanta is not limited to one class and that the scope of influence of most leaders is limited to relatively specific policy areas. Economic dominants are seen as relatively unimportant in community decision making although many of the attributed leaders are men of some wealth and status.

Jennings concludes that Hunter was wrong in his assessment of the power structure of Atlanta and that this error can be traced largely to the methodology used, specifically Hunter's failure to consider governmental decisions in formulating his image of the power structure. Jennings argues that Atlanta's power structure, rather than being characterized by a cohesive ruling elite of economic dominants, is better pictured as a series of more or less competitive coalitions, some of which involve economic dominants and some of which do not.

Jennings, M. Kent. "Public Administrators and Community Decision Making," *Administrative Science Quarterly* 8 (June 1963) 18-43.

Community leaders in Atlanta, Georgia, and Raleigh, North Carolina, are identified by a panel of "knowledgeables" in each community. It is observed that this method of selecting community leadership understates the influence of public administrators in community decision making. By examining a series of issues in each community the author concludes that while the scope of influence of public administrators is somewhat narrower (in most instances) than that of the nominated leaders, administrators do play a significant role in community decision making.

Kammerer, Gladys M.; Farris, Charles D.; Degrove, John M.; and Clubok, Alfred B. *The Urban Political Community: Profiles in Town Politics* (Boston: Houghton-Mifflin & Co., 1963).

The authors examine, in case study style, eight Florida communities which range in population from 5,000 to 60,000. They focus their attention on city elections and especially on the role of the city manager in town politics. While no systematic effort is made by the authors to describe and compare the community power structures of the individual cities and to account for whatever differences exist, some generalizations about the nature of politics and the distribution of influence are presented: (1) city managers tend to play a major role in the community decision-making process; (2) often the struggles for power among competing interests in the communities studied centered about efforts to dismiss a city manager or to hire a new one; (3) rapid population growth seemed to be associated with greater political conflict within the community, especially when this growth was the result of an influx of persons with new expectations, interests, or style of life, i.e., when new residents are from different economic groups, different social classes, and different ages; (4) the authors discern a shift in their communities from more monopolistic to more competitive politics; smaller cities were more likely to be monopolistic; and (5) in five of the eight communities, banks played a central role in the organization of a political clique; this was not true in the poorest community, nor in a community which depended on the economic institutions of a larger adjacent city; (6) developers and realtors were especially ubiquitous in the politics of the communities studied and they often forged political alliances with small businessmen in the local Chamber of Commerce. However, the role of the developers is seen as a passing phenomemon, lasting only so long as the developer has a direct pecuniary interest in city policies such as zoning and building standards; and (7) other community groups active in politics in several or all of the communities studied were retirees and tourism interests.

Kammeyer, Kenneth. "A Comparative Study of Decision Making in Rural Communities," *Rural Sociology* 27 (September 1962) 294-302.

This is a comparative study of 110 rural communities in which a vote had been taken on a school district reorganization plan which would have had the effect of discontinuing the local high school. Relationships were found between several demographic and ecological variables and the degree to which community members expressed opposition to discontinuance of the local high school.

Kammeyer, Kenneth. "Community Homogeneity and Decision Making," *Rural Sociology* 28 (September 1963) 238-45.

This is a further report on the study reviewed above. Contrary to expectations, ethnically homogeneous communities displayed less opposition to loss of their high schools then did heterogeneous communities.

Kimball, S., and Pearsall, M. *The Talladega Story* (University of Alabama Press, 1954).

Kimbrough, Ralph B. *Political Power and Educational Decision Making* (Chicago: Rand McNally, 1964).

Reviews:
  LaNoue, George R., *American Political Science Review* 59 (December 1965) 1004-05.

From his study of educational decision making in four counties, the largest of which has a population of 70,000, the author concludes that actual power in these communities is not as broadly diffused as one would be led to believe by observing who held positions of leadership in formal institutions and in community associations. He argues that educators can get more done by finding the informal power holders and by aligning with them rather than working with those who hold formal positions in institutions which presumably wield power. A chapter is devoted to a critical view of the community power literature published from 1953 to the time the manuscript was submitted.

Klapp, Orrin, and Padgett, Vincent L. "Power Structure and Decision Making in a Mexican Border City," *American Journal of Sociology* 65 (January 1960) 400-406.

The distribution of influence in Tijuana, Mexico (population 160,000) is identified by a panel of "knowledgeables." Businessmen are found to be the most frequently identified "top influentials" but they do not form a cohesive elite in that they were often unaware of the activities of other businessman. Politicians with labor support and religious groups were also seen as influential. A number of important community issues are seen as being resolved from outside the community through the intervention in local affairs on the part of the national party leadership. Various patterns of community action are also described.

The authors view the distribution of influence in Tijuana as largely unstructured and liken it to the formulation developed by Norton Long in his description of the community as an ecology of games. The authors also comment on the impact on the distribution of influence of cultural differences in Mexico and the United States.

Kuroda, Yasumasa. "Political Role Attributions and Dynamics in a Japanese Community," *Public Opinion Quarterly* 29 (Winter 1965-66) 602-13.

In this study of a community of 16,500 people located near Tokyo, the author approaches the study of political influence by examining the kinds of roles citizens play at the local level. Data was collected from interviews with a sample of one-thirtieth of the registered voters in the community, together with reputational analysis of top leaders. The study was designed to replicate that of Agger and Ostrom ("Political Participation in a Small Community"), thus enabling cross-cultural comparisons. The study shows differences from and similarities with structures in American communities. The author is encouraged to find that basic hypotheses drawn from the literature on American community power are borne out in the analysis and that the same techniques can be used effectively in comparative research.

Lindquist, J.H. "An Occupational Analysis of Local Politics: Syracuse, New York, 1880-1959," *Sociology and Social Research* 49 (April 1965) 343-54.

The author examines the occupations of persons who held elective or appointive political office or position in political parties over an eighty-year period in Syracuse, New York. He finds that changes in the occupational and economic structure of the community were not greatly related to changes in the nature of control of local politics. Throughout the entire period the positions of influence under study were controlled or dominated by local businessmen.

Lindquist, John H. "Socioeconomic Status and Political Participation," *Western Political Quarterly* 17 (December 1964) 608-14.

In this study of the socioeconomic status of office-holders in Syracuse, New York, over the eighty-year period 1880-1959, the author finds that those of high socioeconomic status are disproportionately represented in public and party office. Furthermore, over the period there is a clearly marked trend toward greater selection of office-holders from this group and a concomitant drop in office-holding on the part of members of the lower socioeconomic classes. Thus, it appears that, unless Syracuse is unique, local government has been and is increasingly controlled by the upper classes. As long as this is the case, the rest of society is dependent upon the social conscience of the upper classes for the promotion of general interests. The author asserts, however, that this social conscience has not always contributed to the best interests of the majority of the population.

Lowry, Richie P. "Leadership Interaction in Group Consciousness and Social Change," *The Pacific Sociological Review* 7 (Spring 1964) 22-29.

The author observes that two major defects in studies of community power structures are: (1) they tend to be largely particularistic and idiosyncratic in approach and in the type and kind of data collected and analyzed and (2) they rarely employ general theories of social and cultural change which would facilitate comparative analysis and which would further permit the application of the findings to other types of social systems. To deal with these problems he proposes: (1) to utilize a modified version of Marxian theory of change; (2) to utilize a general theory of community leadership interaction taken from Robert Merton and (3) to examine a specific community setting.

Utilizing the research technique of participant observation, for a period of five years the author studies a northern California city called "Micro City" (Chico, California) which services a population of about 35,000. Micro City is described as Protestant, white collar and middle class. Three major leadership groups were identified: locals, cosmopolitans, and business-realty-insurance coalition. The basis for each of these groups is not economic or social in origin or nature but is rather the particular orientation of the group to community issues and problems. The struggle for influence, in short, is not class based.

Until recently, politics in "Micro City" had been controlled by locals whose influence was largely latent. Recent demographic and technological change brought younger, more urban-orientated individuals to the community and this change resulted in increasing contacts between "Micro City" and a larger society and created a feeling of frustration, apathy and alienation in all of the leadership groups. Conflict over issues has become more hostile and tense and all of the groups have a sense of powerlessness to cope with community problems. Cosmopolitan leaders set a style and mission for the community but they did not exercise much direct influence. The business-realty-insurance coalition emerged as the group which sets public policies in the city. The sense of alienation and frustration that each group felt led to the development of new group consciousness in the leadership. To relieve their anxiety they sought to establish a sense of solidarity in mission and to translate these feelings into action. However, such action tends to be taken on behalf of the leadership group itself rather than for other, dispossessed groups in the community.

Lowry, Richie P. *Who's Running This Town? Community Leadership and Social Change* (New York: Harper and Row, 1965).

Reviews:

Salisbury, Robert H., *Midwest Journal of Political Science* 10 (May 1966) 246-48.

Miller, Delbert C., *American Sociological Review* 31 (June 1966) 421-22.

Hartman, John J., *Sociology Quarterly* 7 (Fall 1966) 524-25.

Gist, Noel P., *Social Forces* 45 (September 1966) 130-31.

Rosenthal, Donald B., *American Journal of Sociology* 72 (January 1967) 432.

Based on first-hand observations over time, the author concludes that "Micro City," (Chico, California, which services a population of about 35,000) was dominated by a relatively small and relatively cohesive segment of the business community. However, politics are not class oriented. He argues that commitment to the status quo is the norm in Micro City and is the result of an acute failure or alienation of leadership elements in the community. He develops six abstract types of leaders, which builds on Merton's local-cosmopolitan dichotomy.

Lynd, Robert S., and Lynd, Helen M. *Middletown* (New York: Harcourt, Brace and Co., 1929).

This study of Muncie, Indiana (population 35,000) was among the first efforts to understand, in depth, the culture of an American community aand how that culture is affected by and shapes the lives of the community's people. Using a social-anthropological approach, the authors sought to examine all aspects of life in the community. In this volume they are not explicitly concerned with the nature of the community power structure but they do indicate that business classes dominate the working classes. More direct concern with the use of political and social power in Muncie is contained in the follow-up study, entitled *Middletown in Transition.*

Lynd, Robert S., and Lynd, Helen M. *Middletown in Transition* (New York: Harcourt, Brace and Co., 1937).

In this follow-up to their earlier study of Muncie, Indiana (population 35,000), based on a restudy of the community during the 1930's, the authors deal more explicitly than they did in their earlier research with the question of how community power is distributed and utilized. Consistent with the more general findings of their earlier study, they conclude that Muncie is controlled by a small business elite which in turn is dominated by one family. It is asserted that the influence of this family reaches into all areas of community affairs, both public and private.

Martin, Roscoe C.; Munger, Frank J., et. al. *Decision in Syracuse: A Metropolitan Action Study* (Bloomington, Indiana: Indiana University Press, 1961).
Reviews:
Knepper, David W., *Journal of Politics* 24 (August 1962) 622-23.
Rogers, David, *American Sociological Review* 27 (September 1962) 267-68.
Dvorin, Eugene P., *Western Political Quarterly* 15 (September 1962) 564-65.
The distribution of influence in Syracuse, New York and its immediate environs is discovered by examining the disposition of twenty-two cases of points of decision or action which occurred during a twenty-five-year period. According to the authors, these twenty-two situations represent "all significant action" undertaken during the study period. They reject the possibility that the structure of influence in Syracuse is monolithic in character. Instead they see various groups or coalitions of leaders exercising influence within distinct decision areas.

A number of differentiated roles played by persons active in the decision-making process are identified. These roles are: (1) initiators (idea men); (2) experts (policy formulators); (3) publicists; (4) influentials (persons *believed* to hold the power of decision); (5) brokers and (6) transmitters of power. The findings are utilized to develop a relatively abstract model of decision making on the metropolitan level.

Martindale, Don, and Hanson, R. Galen. *Small Town and the Nation: The Conflict of Local and Translocal Forces* (Westport, Connecticut: Greenwood Publishing Corporation, 1969).

Reviews:

Field, Donald R., *Rural Sociology* 35 (September 1970) 427-28.

Johnson, Ronald, *American Sociological Review* 36 (April 1971) 370.

This study is an examination of the disintegration of the social structure of a small town — Benson, a town of 4,000 people in west-central Minnesota — when confronted by the culture of the larger society. The authors describe in detail the specific conflicts arising from the erosion of local autonomy by national politics, media, and outside commercial-industrial interests. Data was collected from participant observation, documentary and published sources and self-administered questionnaires completed by three different samples of respondents: "Old-style" Bensonites were selected from persons whose occupations were local in nature; "new-style" Bensonites, from those whose occupations were translocal; and, as a control group, ex-Bensonites, selected from persons who had once lived in Benson. The findings confirmed with minor exceptions the central hypothesis that the conflict between old ideals and contemporary realities is present in all major areas of Benson's institutional life, and, specifically, that: (1) the lines of tension between local and nonlocal forces are discernible in the economy; (2) the structure of power and influence is polarized in terms of local and nonlocal interests; and (3) the major lines of stress in Benson's institutions of socialization arise from the conflict of local and nonlocal interests.

McClain, Jackson M., and Highshaw, Robert B. *Dixie City: A Study in Decision Making* (Birmingham, Alabama: Bureau of Public Administration, University of Alabama, 1962).

McKee, James B. "Status and Power in the Industrial Community: A Comment on Drucker's Thesis," *American Journal of Sociology* 58 (January 1953) 364-70.

Decision making in Lorain, Ohio (population 50,000) is examined over a period of time. It is concluded that the distribution of influence in the community is widespread. The influence of business elites in governmental affairs was limited. The community's economy was dominated by a single steel-producing industry and McKee argues that his findings are in conflict with Peter Drucker's thesis that the status and power hierarchy of the corporation is transferred to the society. It is found that labor, in coalition with ethnic groups, the Democratic party and the Catholic church, exerts dominant control over political decision making. However, the power of labor is attenuated by its needs to achieve greater levels of legitimacy in the minds of the community as a whole.

Merton, Robert K. "Patterns of Influence: A Study of Interpersonal Influence and of Communications Behavior in a Local Community," in Paul F. Lazarsfeld and Frank N. Stanton, eds, *Communication Research in 1948-49* (New York: Harper and Row, 1949) pp. 180-219.

In order to identify opinion leaders in "Rovere," a suburb of 11,000 residents in an eastern state, a panel of eighty-six informants knowledgeable about community affairs was asked to indicate whose advice they personally valued most. The fifty-seven persons who were nominated four or more times were considered to be "influentials" and thirty of these were interviewed. Influentials were then classified into dichotomous categories of "locals" and "cosmopolitans." The author asserts that objective attributes of the persons nominated as influentials, such as education, occupation, social status, etc. do not suffice in determining interpersonal influence. Interpersonal influence is regarded as a chain of interaction with high influentials influencing middle influentials who influence low influentials who influence the rank and file. However, interpersonal influence "from the bottom up" is also found.

Cosmopolitans and locals are distinguished in terms of their orientation toward the world, locals being more parochial and cosmopolitans viewing themselves as integral parts of the larger world. The influence of locals depends not on expertise but on interpersonal relationships; cosmopolitans, on the other hand, are influential in the community mainly because of their skills and experience.

Patterns of influence are classified as monomorphic and polymorphic. Monomorphic influence refers to influence related to more or less specific issues and tends to characterize top influentials and cosmopolitans. Polymorphic influence, that is influence on a relatively broad range of questions, tends to characterize locals and middle and lower influentials. Merton concludes that more decisions in the community may be affected by those ranking in the middle and low ranges of influence because there are more of them and because those at the top may be concerned and influential only with respect to a narrow range of issues. Merton concludes that, "positions in the class, power and prestige hierarchies contribute to the potential for interpersonal influence but do not determine the extent to which influence actually occurs."

Miller, Delbert C. "Decision-Making Cliques in Community Power Structures: A Comparative Study of an American and an English City." *American Journal of Sociology* 64 (November 1958) 299-310.

Top influentials in Bristol, England and Seattle, Washington (each with a population of about 450,000) were identified by 10 "expert" raters from among a lengthy list of leaders nominated by "knowledgeables" representing nine institutional sectors in each community. Those persons with the greatest attributed power were identified as "key influentials." These findings were contrasted with Hunter's findings in Atlanta, Georgia.

It was found that in each of the two cities studied, there was greater communication among influentials of different status than Hunter found. As compared to top influentials in general, the key influentials were more likely to participate in a number of organizations and to hold common membership with other key influentials in one or more organizations. Businessmen dominated the group of identified influentials but did not wield general influence over a broad range of issues. In general influentials from all community sectors tended to focus on specific types of issues. The power structure of Bristol is seen as less stable, less structured, and more diffused than that found in Seattle.

Miller, Delbert C. *International Community Power Structures: Comparative Studies of Four World Cities* (Bloomington, Indiana: Indiana University Press, 1970).
Reviews:
Clark, Terry N., *American Sociological Review* 36 (February 1971) 149.

This study seeks to identify and compare the power structure in Seattle, Bristol, Lima and Cordova. Top and key leaders are identified by combined use of the positional, decisional and reputational methods, with priority given to the reputational approach because it reveals those aspects of the social structure which are relatively stable. In addition, this technique was applied to ranking organizations and community institutions, the first such application, in the author's opinion. The theoretical framework is based on Form and Miller's system model, which views the community power structure as a pattern of interacting parts: the dominant institutions in society put their stamp on the institutional power structure of the community, from which the community power complex – a power arrangement among groups and organizations – emerges. It is assumed that top and key influentials "will occur in number and influence proportionate to the power distribution of institutions in the institutionalized power structure of the community."

Having compared Bristol and Seattle and then Cordova and Lima in depth, the author compares all four cities and finds that the system model proves to be useful as a guide; it points out the importance and relationship of institutions, associations, and leaders. The power ranking of the top three local institutions varied over the four cities as follows: Seattle – Business, Local Government, Labor; Bristol – Local Government, Business, Political Parties; Cordova – Religion, Business, Local Government; and Lima – Local Government, Political Parties, Business.

The author found that in none of the cities was there a single solidary elite structure or hierarchical dominance based on one institutional structure. Thus, all four cities approximate the cone or ring model, characterized by a heterogeneous business sector, countervailing powers (labor, church, second political party), and autonomy of institutional sectors. There is a pool of top and key influentials, organizations and institutions which interact to produce various patterns of influence in community decision making. Miller found that in all cities, however, there are key influentials to whom all leaders look when salient issues arise.

Note: Chapter 10 of this book is an adaptation of a study of Cordova by Delbert C. Miller with the assistance of Eva Chamorro and Juan Carlos Agulla, "Community Power Perspectives and Role Definitions of North American Executives in an Argentine Community," *Administrative Science Quarterly* 10 (December 1965) 364-80.

Miller, Delbert C. "Industry and Community Power Structure: A Comparative Study of an English and an American City," *American Sociological Review* 23 (February 1958) 9-15.

Influentials in Bristol, England and Seattle, Washington, each with a population of about 450,000, are identified by a panel of knowledgeable "judges" from various institutional sectors in each city. The power structure in Seattle is seen as more hierarchial and dominated by businessmen. In comparison, power in Bristol is more diffused and is more likely to be exercised by people who hold formal positions of power in governmental councils and agencies. It is noted that even in Seattle the degree of influence wielded by businessmen was less than that which Hunter found in Atlanta, Georgia.

The reasons for the difference in the structure of community power in Bristol and Seattle are explained by: (1) different occupational prestige systems, i.e., businessmen in America enjoy more status than they do in England; and (2) norms call for government to play a more positive and more autonomous role in community decision making in England than is the case in America (for example, pressure on the Bristol Council is considered bad taste); and (3) the broad representation on the city council in England (there are 112 members from twenty-eight wards) which provides the various groups in the community with access to the decision-making process.

Miller, Delbert C. "Town and Gown: The Power Structure of a University Town," *American Journal of Sociology* 68 (January 1963) 432-43.

A panel of persons with good knowledge of community affairs in Bloomington, Indiana (population 31,000) was asked to nominate community influentials. Those nominated are themselves asked to rank, in terms of their influence, those nominated by the first panel and others they might add to the list. It is found that businessmen dominate the community power structure but that the newspaper, government officials and persons involved in education also have influence in community decision making. Organizations which are ranked as most powerful are dominated by businessmen with the exception of the League of Women Voters. University administrators play some role in the decision-making process although only two of the twelve most influential persons in the community are identified with the university. University faculty play only a minor role in community affairs and the author attributes this to the more cosmopolitan nature of the academic community. University faculty are more likely to identify with the problems of the nation and the world than with the problems of the local community. (This article also appeared in the *Ohio Valley Sociologist,* 1961, under the same title.)

Miller, Delbert C., and Dirksen, James L. "The Identification of Visible, Concealed and Symbolic Leaders in a Small Indiana City: A Replication of the Bonjean-Noland Study of Burlington, North Carolina," *Social Forces* 43 (May 1965) 548-55.

A panel of community activists was asked to identify the leaders of this Indiana city of 31,000 residents (Bloomington, Indiana). These nominated leaders were in turn asked to evaluate the role played by themselves and other nominated leaders in actual decision making. The evaluations of those ranked highest in the initial ratings were weighted more heavily. Those ranked equally by key influentials and lower order leaders were classified, according to the Bonjean-Noland formula, as visible leaders. Those who were seen as influential by key influentials and not by others were called concealed leaders. Those persons, such as the mayor, who were identified as leaders by lower ranked influentials but not by key influentials were classified as "symbolic leaders."

Visible leaders were businessmen except for a judge who was fairly wealthy. Concealed leaders were business or professional men but were not, as a group, as wealthy as visible leaders. Symbolic leaders were from a diversity of occupational backgrounds. The findings in Bloomington are compared with those in Burlington and the existing differences are discussed.

Mills, C. Wright. "The Middle Classes in Middle-Sized Cities," *American Sociological Review* 11 (December 1946) 520-29.

On the basis of his study of a midwest city of 60,000 in population, Mills concludes that community affairs are dominated by big businessmen in this community. Initiative in community projects was taken by the Chamber of Commerce, which was dominated by big business. Small businessmen often "fronted" for big business and identified with that stratum. White-collar persons were not very active in community affairs but tended to represent a middle ground between the interests of the business community and that of labor. Mills concludes that community politics is becoming increasingly polarized with the ideology and politics of business on the one hand and of the working classes on the other becoming increasingly rigid.

Mills, C. Wright, and Ulmer, Melvin. *Small Business and Civic Welfare: Report on Smaller War Plants Corporation to the Special Committee to Study Problems of American Small Business* (Senate Document No. 135, 79th Congress, Second Session, Washington, D.C., 1946).

Six American cities of varying degrees of big business dominance of the industrial sector are studied to determine the relationship between the quality of life in the community and the degree to which the economy is dominated by one, or a few, large industries. The authors conclude that there is more social and cultural diversity and more civic spirit in communities whose economy is primarily small business in character. They ranked each community in terms of the "index of civic goodness" developed by E.L. Thorndike which measures civic welfare in terms of 37 different items. The civic welfare of small business cities was found to be noticeably higher than the civic welfare rating achieved by communities whose economic structure was dominated by big business.

Norbeck, Edward. *Pineapple Town: Hawaii* (Berkeley: University of California Press, 1959).

Reviews:

Murphy, Thomas D., *Annals* 327 (January 1960) 160.

Glick, C.E., *American Sociological Review* 25 (February 1960) 139.

This is a study of the social structure of a racially diverse "company town" on a 10,000-acre pineapple plantation, located on the comparatively isolated island of Molakai.

Olmsted, Donald W. "Organizational Leadership and Social Structure in a Small City," *American Sociological Review* 19 (June 1954) 273-81.

A small panel of "knowledgeables" in Red Wing, Minnesota (population of 10,000) identified community leaders in both 1943 and 1949. Other leaders selected during both years by a random sample of citizens and by a special sample of labor leaders were added to the list formulated by the "knowledgeables." It was found that leaders participated in community organizations much more frequently than the community sample and that this was even more pronounced in 1949 than in 1943. The specific leaders identified in 1943 differed substantially from those identified in 1949. The leaders in the citizen sample were ranked according to their degree of social participation. Community leaders tended to hold overlapping memberships in key community organizations and this network of informal contact was the basis for a key leader subsystem which led to a substantial amount of integration of the social system. The author concludes that social participation gives an objective basis for assessing patterns of leadership in voluntary organizations and that voluntary organizational leadership constitutes an important part of the social organization of the community as a whole.

Oommen, T.K. "Rural Community Power Structure in India," *Social Forces* 49 (December 1970) 226-39.

In this study of four small Indian villages (ranging in size from 55 to 91 households) in the state of Rajastam, the author explores the power structure with the objective of understanding the relationship between community characteristics and power dispersion. The author first identified the "power pool" – all persons involved in the "power arena" – by listing those who occupy formal power positions, by interviewing the head of each household to find out who is considered to be the respondent's leaders, and by observing the decision-making process in village organizations. The importance of variables such as community size, caste structure, occupational variations, and educational and organizational innovations for the dispersion of power are then examined.

Parenton, Vernon J., and Pellegrin, Roland J. "Social Structure and the Leadership Factor in a Negro Community in South Louisiana," *Phylon* 17 (First Quarter 1956) 74-78.

A Negro community of less than 500 persons in Bertrandville, Louisiana, provides the environment for this study. The community is characterized by substantial poverty and the population is more than 50 percent Catholic. Leadership rested almost solely with the white priests that serve this community. The community is examined over an extensive period of time and it is found that in recent years efforts at economic upgrading and general community betterment have been successful. Improvement of the social situation in a relatively hostile environment was possible because the leadership provided by the priests was relatively immune to common modes of attack often utilized by the white power structure.

Pellegrin, Roland J., and Coates, Charles. "Absentee-Owned Corporations and Community Power Structure," *American Journal of Sociology* 61 (March 1956) 413-19.

This study of "Big Town" (Baton Rouge, Louisiana, population about 200,000), focuses on the role of absentee-owned corporations which dominate the economy of this city in community decision making. The authors note an absence of a well-defined leadership group which takes initiative for solving community problems. Because of the leadership vacuum, the local managers of the absentee-owned corporations hold a veto power over community projects.

Perrucci, Robert, and Pilisuk, Marc. "Leaders and Ruling Elites: The Inter-organizational Bases of Community Power," *American Sociological Review* 35 (December 1970) 1040-57.

In a midwestern community of 50,000 population, the authors identified from a comprehensive list of organizations and leaders a group of twenty-six individuals who held high positions in four or more organizations — designated as inter-organizational leaders (IOL). In order to examine the importance of inter-organizational ties for community power, these leaders were matched with organizational leaders (OL) in one to three organizations on the basis of similar primary vocational identification. These fifty-two leaders were interviewed and their influence analyzed in terms of both reputed and issue-specific power. IOL are more likely than the OL to (1) be identified as involved in past community issues of major proportions; (2) be identified as having a general reputation for power; (3) be similar in their views on community issues; (4) see each other socially; and (5) be identified as powerful from sociometric power choices. These procedures, the authors feel, permit testing for the existence of a ruling elite which could not be determined within the framework of existing elitist and pluralist theory. They conclude that a ruling elite does exist, and although it is not necessarily interested or involved in every community decision, this group has resources "necessary to assure an outcome favorable to its interests" when its common values are at stake in a community dispute.

Pfautz, Harold W. "The Power Structure of the Negro Sub-Community: A Case Study and a Comparative View," *Phylon* 23 (Summer 1962) 156-66.

The leaders of the Negro community of Providence, Rhode Island, which in 1950 comprised 3.3 percent of the city's total population of about 250,000, were identified by a panel of ten "knowledgeable" persons. Those identified were asked to rate each other and ultimately a list of the sixteen top leaders was formulated. The power structure is seen as split into three factions, each with differing attitudes on the way civil rights should be secured and how much effort should be devoted to that end. Those in the middle, while numerically fewer, were seen as the most influential.

Negro leaders are seen as relatively ineffective in dealing with the larger community.

The author suggests that the reputational approach may have greater validity in the study of out-group sub-communities because of the greater interaction among elites in such sub-communities as compared to the larger social system. In the case of Negroes, the centrality of the race question means that elites are not fragmented in terms of issue specialization as they often are in the community as a whole.

Pinard, Maurice. "Structural Attachments and Political Support in Urban Politics: The Case of Fluoridation Referendums," *American Journal of Sociology* 68 (March 1963) 513-26.

This article tests the hypothesis that the adoption or rejection of fluoridation referendums, as well as the degree of unanimity, is a function of the structural integration of the community; the outcome is a function of the attachments of community members to their power elites and the strength of interconnectedness between members of the community and the elite. Data from 262 communities which had considered fluoridating the water system was analyzed, and it was found that the size of communities, their rates of growth, their ethnic and racial composition, the condition of their labor market, and their occupational and power structures are all important features of the social system that influence community decisions. Specifically, it was found that when elites were small and united the likelihood of success is greatest.

Present, Phillip Edward. "Defense Contracting and Community Leadership: A Comparative Analysis," *Southwestern Social Science Quarterly* 48 (December 1967) 399-410.

This study of two relatively isolated southern California communities — "Elmwood," population 10,000, and "Centerville," population, 30,000 — seeks to explore the relationship between community politics and change in the economic setting. Specifically, the article focuses on the relationship between community leadership structures and defense contracting. The findings suggest that defense contracting, whose introduction was the only new economic force in the previously isolated communities, caused changes in the composition, size and rate of turnover in the leadership structures.

Presthus, Robert. *Men at the Top: A Study in Community Power* (New York: Oxford University Press, 1964).

Reviews:

Long, Norton, *American Journal of Sociology* 70 (January 1965) 482-83.

Booth, David A., *Journal of Politics* 27 (February 1965) 237-39.

Kellstadt, Lyman, "Atlanta to Oretown: Identifying Community Elites," *Public Administration Review* 25 (June 1965) 161-68.

Dreyer, Edward C., *Western Political Quarterly* 18 (June 1965) 412-13.

D'Antonio, William V., *American Sociological Review* 30 (February 1965) 157-58.

Schulze, Robert O. *Social Forces* (October 1964) 110.

The structure of power is identified in two small New York communities (populations 6,000 and 8,500) using both participation in decision making and reputation for leadership as criteria for identifying community leaders. Five types of decisions were studied in each community and four were common to both. The author concludes that both the "decisional" and "reputational" approaches to the study of community power are useful in that each serves as a check on the accuracy of the other in assessing the various elements of community influence.

The power structure of each community is seen as dominated by a very small number of citizens. Two relatively discrete decision-making systems were found: (1) a "private" system in which economic leaders dominated, and (2) a public system in which political leaders had general control. Because their basis of influence in the total power structure is more stable, economic leaders are seen as enjoying greater continuity in the power structure.

Viewing the power structure of each city as a whole, economic leaders enjoyed somewhat more power than political leaders in one community (Edgewood) while the reverse was true in the other community (Riverview). The somewhat different patterns of leadership in the community are explored in detail and some differences in the economic and social structures of the two communities are advanced as possible causal explanations. The book also includes a relatively extensive review of the literature on community power with special emphasis on the methodological problems involved.

Rabinovitz, Francine F. *City Politics and Planning* (New York: Atherton Press, 1969).

Reviews:
Williams, Oliver P., *American Political Science Review* 64 (June 1970) 640.
Palmer, David, *Western Political Quarterly* 22 (December 1969) 980.

In this study, certain characteristics of six New Jersey communities — organization of the planning operation, variation in the role of the planner, and political system differences measured along a pluralist-elitist continuum — are examined in an attempt to explain the effectiveness of planning. The measurement of effectiveness is based on the ratings of a panel of informed judges. The author then constructs a typology of political systems taking into account the distribution of power, the political culture and outputs of the political system. From the analysis, four system types are generated: cohesive, executive-centered, competitive and fragmented.

Rabinovitz, Francine F. "Politics, Personality and Planning," *Public Administration Review* 27 (March 1967) 18-24.

Differences in the nature of decision making in communities are identified and the implications of this diversity for the political role of urban planners are discussed.

Rhyne, Edwin H. "Political Parties and Decision Making in Three Southern Counties," *American Political Science Review* 52 (December 1958) 1091-1107.

Political leaders in three southern counties were identified by community influentials who were selected by the author. The three counties studied were similar in socioeconomic and demographic characteristics but differed in the degree of party competition as measured by competition for partisan county offices. Those who hold county or party offices are compared to the power elite in each case. Officeholders' attitudes toward the electorate and the types of issues that become campaign issues are studied.

The author concludes that there is no necessary relationship between party competition in a community and the accountability of the local political elite to the citizenry. The author suggests that among the conditions one must examine in addition to party competition are: (1) the involvement of public discussion of current issues in electoral contests; (2) the degree to which parties are involved in the local decision-making process; (3) the closeness of party competition and (4) the relationship between parties at various levels of government.

Rossi, Peter H. "The Organizational Structure of an American Community," in Amatai Etzioni, ed., *Complex Organizations: A Sociological Reader* (New York: Holt, Rinehart and Winston, 1961) pp. 301-12.

The author conducted personal interviews with about fifty businessmen and community leaders, and with fifteen members of the general population, in "Mediana," a midwest industrial city of about 45,000 population. Both formal and informal policy making in Mediana was dominated by the business community. Labor's role in public and political office was very minor. Businessmen who hold public office are largely locals and persons who have resided in the community for some time. The role of politician has low status in the business community as a whole. Much of the identification of issues and the development of public policy actually takes place in voluntary civic organizations and through the Chamber of Commerce in which the managers of absentee-owned enterprise play a greater role. The author suggests that in American communities generally there is a status gap between the officials of local government and the local elites of wealth, intellect and status. Thus, unofficial community organizations serve to redress the local imbalance of power by giving the elite of status and wealth important sectors of community life to control.

Salisbury, Robert H. "St. Louis Politics: Relationships Among Interests, Parties, and Governmental Structure," *Western Political Quarterly* 13 (June 1960) 498-507.

Based on his long-term study of St. Louis politics, the author concludes that the holders of political power in that city can be grouped into two broadly based coalitions: one comprised of downtown business interests and upper-middle and middle-income residents; and the other made up of some elements of labor, Negroes, local businessmen and lower-income residents. However, within these broad coalitions, cohesion is weak and on many issues it does not exist. He argues that the fragmentation of political influence is related in part to the fragmentation of political institutions both within the city and in the county of which St. Louis is a part. He finds that governmental structure has a direct bearing on the way political conflict is manifested, and on its intensity and scope, but that interest group patterns appear to be more critical.

Sayre, Wallace S., and Kaufman, Herbert. *Governing New York City: Politics in the Metropolis* (New York: Russell Sage Foundation, 1960).
Reviews:
McGoldrick, Joseph D., *American Political Science Review* 54 (September 1960) 733-35.
Ascher, Charles S., *Annals* 333 (January 1961) 178-79.

Long, Norton E., "New York: Competition Without Chaos," *Public Administration Review* 21 (Winter 1961).

Cleveland, Frederic N., *Journal of Politics* 23 (May 1961) 385-87.

Wilson, James Q., American *Journal of Sociology* 66 (November 1960) 300-301.

To determine the distribution of political influence in New York City, the authors examine the election process, the distribution of city administrative positions, and the outcome of specific issues. In addition, over a period of time they study the activities of groups and institutions which they identify as key elements in the political process. The major participants in decision making are: administrators of line agencies and other key bureaucrats, special authorities and certain agencies, parties and nongovernmental groups, the courts, officials of other governments, the city council, the Board of Estimates, and the mayor's office. The distribution of political influence is characterized as a series of decision centers which provide multiple opportunities for political access, each of which is surrounded by groups especially concerned with its decisions. Each decision center has its core and peripheral influential. These decision centers are relatively autonomous from one another and there exists no mechanism or center of power by which these various decision centers may be drawn together should the common interest so require. Decisions affecting two or more power centers are arrived at by mutual accommodation between the governmental and private groups willing to contest the issue.

Schaffer, Albert, and Schaffer, Ruth Connor. *Woodruff: A Study of Community Decision Making* (Chapel Hill: The University of North Carolina Press, 1970).

Reviews:

Davis, Adam Clarke, *Social Forces* 49 (December 1970) 318-19.

This is a study of the response of a city, Woodruff (population, 20,957 in 1960) and surrounding township (population, 25,959) to ecological and social problems confronting them since World War II, and the interation between the two governmental units. Decision making and policy formation concerning questions of area development — especially the promotion of business and industry and proposals for annexation or consolidation — are analyzed in terms of the structure of community influence in the city and township and the "decision patterns" — expansionist vs. restrictionist strategies — for dealing with change which developed over time. The delineation of patterns of community influence are based upon a combination of reputational and positional approaches as well as the close examination of the decision-making system afforded by the authors' seven-year residence in and intimate involvement with the civic affairs of Woodruff. The interplay between leadership structure and decision patterns in response to forces of change is the focus of the book. Although combination of the two governmental units would have increased the system's capacity to function effectively, status incongruence between the influentials in the city (dominated by well-to-do old families) and the township (from new families and often leaders of blue-collar organizations) reinforced the persistence of the "restrictionist" pattern among leaders in the city and induced township leaders to actively oppose merger. Through nondecision and negative decision making in the city and opposition to merger in the township, the influentials in both were successful in maintaining two separate governments. Although the distribution of power was pluralistic in both city and township, the authors conclude that influentials have largely had their way. This is due to "the continuity and exercise of decision-making patterns, not the concentration of power."

Schulze, Robert O. "The Bifurcation of Power in a Satellite City," in Morris Janowitz, ed., *Community Political Systems* (Glencoe, Illinois: The Free Press, 1961) pp. 19-80.

This study represents an elaboration of an earlier article by the author which reports the changing patterns of influence in "Cibola" (Ypsilanti, Michigan, population 20,000). For the period 1823-1955, the author examines the role of economic dominants (economic dominants are identified by position in major industries and commercial establishments or by property ownership) in appointed and elected public office. He concludes that the advent of absentee ownership of industry in Cibola was associated with an increasing tendency of economic dominants to eschew formal roles in political institutions. He finds that economic dominants remain active (but less so than before) in private community civic organizations. He goes further to argue that the appearance of prestige and wealthy persons in the decision-making process may be the result of cooptation by political leaders who seek the legitimacy that the economic dominants can afford. Thus it may be that economic dominants are often being "used" by political leaders rather than being the manipulators that many other students of community power have inferred. In short, economic dominants may be reluctant participants in political decision making. The author notes, however, that political decision-makers are sensitive to the stake that economic dominants have in decisions which directly affect the latters' interest. The author checks his findings by studying some local issues and finds no reason to change his central thesis.

Schulze, Robert O. "The Role of Economic Dominants in Community Power Structure,"*American Sociological Review* 23 (February 1958) 3-9.

This study is a briefer and earlier version of the analysis discussed in the citation immediately above.

Scoble, Harry. "Leadership Hierarchies and Political Issues in a New England Town," in Morris Janowitz, ed., *Community Political Systems,* (Glencoe, Illinois: The Free Press, 1961) pp. 117-45.

The structure of community leadership in "Yankeetown" (Bennington, Vermont, population 12,500) is identified through the analysis of actual decision making in three issue areas. Participants in the decision-making process were asked to evaluate the power of other participants. It is found that overt activity and incumbency in formal leadership positions and the amount of overt participation are not necessarily correlated with high influence. The author finds some overlap in the leadership in each issue area but concludes that there is no single power structure in the community with general influence in all issue areas. It is concluded that the power of leaders is not greatly higher than the influence of nonleaders. The power of any one leader is seen as fluid and perishable and comprised largely of the capacity to: 1) impede or shape (but not prohibit) the development of certain issues and 2) influence the way in which issues were considered.

Seligman, Lester G. "A Prefatory Study of Leadership Selection in Oregon,"*Western Political Quarterly* 12 (March 1959) 153-67.

Smith, Lincoln. "Political Leadership in a New England Community," *Review of Politics* 17 (July 1955) 392-409.

Political decision making in the town of Brunswick, Maine (population 11,000) is reported as being dominated by two town officials, a "moderator" and "treasurer," both of whom had been elected continuously for 50 years and were economic dominants; one was a banker, the other a lawyer.

Smith, Lincoln. "Power Politics in Brunswick: A Case Study," *Human Organization* 22 (Summer 1963) 152-58.

Smith, Paul A. "The Games of Community Politics," *Midwest Journal of Political Science* 9 (February 1965) 37-60.

In this study of "Mayberg," Iowa (population 20,000) community decision making is conceived as a series of games involving conflicting interests, differential rewards, and understood rules of behavior. Using a random sample of the population and a leadership sample, the author finds that the structure of attributed influence tends to vary from policy area to policy area. It is found that those who are reputed to be general influentials also tend to be economic dominants. Compared to other games, politics has a multiplicity and ambiguity of players and audiences. For the community as a whole politics is not a highly salient game and, by and large, economic dominants do not wield substantial influence in this game. By determining the "rules of the game" through interviews and comparing these rules to a study of decision making relative to nominations of public officials for elective office, the author concludes that participation and influence in local politics can be deduced from the rules and payoffs of the political game. In the concluding section the author develops formal and quantitative models of game theory which he suggests are applicable to the study of local politics.

Smith, Ted C. "The Structuring of Power in a Suburban Community," *Pacific Sociological Review* 3 (Fall 1960) 83-88.

The author hypothesizes that determinative influentials of a community would be persons who not only possess a potential for power but whose activities, relationships and value orientations reflect a commitment to the community. To test this hypothesis he studies a residential suburb in Utah which he calls "Northville" (population 18,000). Community leaders were identified by a panel of "knowledgeables" and these nominations were cross-checked among the nominated influentials themselves. As a result, sixteen persons were selected as "top influentials." All sixteen of the leaders were found to have strong commitment to the community. All but two of these could be categorized as economic elites and all but two were active members of the Mormon church. Thus, economic stake in the community and church membership provided for both a high degree of identification with the community and a substantial amount of integration among the "determinative" influentials. It is postulated that the increasing urbanization of Northville will undermine the economic stake many elites now have in the community itself and will result, therefore, in a greater diffusion of influence. It is concluded that none of the economic elites who were associated with absentee-owned enterprise were part of the community power structure.

Speight, John F. "Community Homogeneity and Consensus on Leadership," *Sociological Quarterly* 9 (Summer 1968) 387-96.

Based on data gathered in personal interviews with rural Negroes in twelve small communities in North Carolina, the author seeks to investigate the relationship between the distribution of influence and the community social structure, specifically the relation between consensus on leadership and community homogeneity of socioeconomic characteristics. Contrary to earlier findings on this question, the author finds that socioeconomic homogeneity is not a necessary or sufficient condition for consensus. He accounts for the difference in his findings and that of many other studies in part by the way in which homogeneity and consensus were conceptualized in the study. In this study homogeneity was conceptualized as a continuum of similarity. A consensus was conceptualized as a continuum of agreement instead of conceptualizing both as either all or nothing variables.

Stewart, Frank A. "A Sociometric Study of Influence in Southtown," *Sociometry* 10 (February 1947) 11-31.

The leaders of "Southern City" (population 6,000) are identified by a cross-sectional sample of 163 of the community citizens. Fifty-five persons are identified as top influentials (on the basis of having been nominated ten or more times). A list of leaders based upon participation in specific organizations is found to correlate weakly with the list of top influentials. Only 39 percent of those nominated as leaders by the leaders themselves are found in the group of top influentials defined by the citizenry. Attributed influence is found to be associated with age, being male, high education and high income levels, as well as high rates of personal interaction with others. Further, top influentials tended to be the individuals mentioned most frequently in the local newspaper. Top influentials could not be characterized as either "locals" or cosmopolitans but included both types.

Stewart, Frank A. "A Study of Influence in Southtown: II," *Sociometry* 10 (August 1947) 273-86.

This article is an extension of the article cited immediately above. The author argues that while influence is most often found among those of higher socioeconomic status, the identification of community influentials must depend upon the identification of individuals rather than social or economic classes. Those most often mentioned as influential are found to be characterized by longer residency in the community, greater satisfaction with the community, knowledge of community leadership and interest in civic affairs. Males are far more often nominated as influentials than females. The author focuses on a description and analysis of the flow of interpersonal influence in the community, which he concludes is not class-bound and is very uneven.

Stinchcombe, Jean L. *Reform and Reaction: City Politics in Toledo* (Belmont, California: Wadsworth Publishing Co., Inc., 1968).

This study seeks to assess the impact of reform institutions — council-manager form of government, nonpartisanship and at-large elections — on community politics and decision making in Toledo, Ohio (population 360,000), one of the few large cities to have these governmental forms. The author concludes that reform institutions — by weakening local party organizations, by accentuating the disunity and detachment of community organizations, by lulling business leaders into indifference, and by inhibiting the participation of unions and minorities — have resulted in an amorphous power structure. There is no dominant elite drawn from business or public leaders. Community organizations rarely initiate policy proposals or precipitate local controversies, nor is there a coalition of actors or groups which tends to prevail in most community issues. Although the participation of lower-income groups and minorities has been restricted, business interests and middle-class residents have received few positive benefits. In conclusion, the author asserts that reform has resulted in governmental paralysis, pervasive disinterest, and diffusion of power.

Stone, Robert C. "Power and Values in Trans-Community Relations" in Bert E. Swanson, ed., *Current Trends in Comparative Community Studies* (Kansas City Community Studies, Incorporated, 1962) pp. 69-80.

The author's conclusions concerning the distribution of power in "Service City," Arizona (population 4,500) are based on data collected through interviews, observation, and analysis of the newspapers in the community over a period of one year. The Chamber of Commerce, the school board, and the city government are seen as dominating local decision making. These groups are also of central importance in linking the community to its external environment.

There is a minimum of overlap among the leaders of these three dominant groups in the community. In short, no small group of people controls all, or even most, major decisions. Rather, the author finds specialized leaders associated with differing community programs; no formal or informal group had integrated these various power centers. However, an ideology common to the three organizations which Stone calls "social free enterprise" is identified. This ideology determines the way in which all of the organizations relate to the outside world. It tends to circumscribe the activities of the local government and the school board and to maximize the flexibility and potential influence of the Chamber of Commerce.

Thometz, Carol Estes. *The Decision-Makers: The Power Structure of Dallas* (Dallas: Southern Methodist University Press, 1963).

Reviews:

Crotty, William J., *Journal of Politics* 26 (August 1964) 940-42.

Hoover, John P., *Western Political Quarterly* 17 (September 1964) 567-77.

Schulze, Robert O., *American Sociological Review* 29 (December 1964) 942-43.

Anton, Thomas J., *American Journal of Sociology* 70 (September 1964) 242.

Erickson, Eugene C., *Social Forces* 43 (May 1965) 595-96.

In this study of Dallas, Texas (population 679,684), decision-makers were located and the structure of influence delineated by use of the reputational approach. Having compiled a list of sixty-seven prominent individuals from a panel of informants, a random sample of twenty-eight names was drawn from the list of reputed leaders for interviewing to judge the relative influence of those on the complete list, to add additional names, and to discuss the process of decision making for particular community issues. Analysis of the findings produced the following generalizations: (1) a unified structure of power composed of men possessing "generalized" influence, i.e., influence in many sectors of community activity, exists in Dallas; (2) the group of influentials is small — seven key, fifty-five top-level, and five second-echelon leaders; (3) 90 percent of the leaders are drawn from commerce, finance and industry with only one employed in government; (4) the leaders are distributed into identifiable strata rather than evenly along a continuum of power; and (5) the power rating of leaders is directly related to their association, socially and in committees; the most influential leaders are better known than less influential leaders, and have participated on committees with more other leaders than have less influential leaders. In specific issues, these decision-makers are highly successful in determining the outcome because of unified effort and organization as well as foresight, thoughtful planning, and effective utilization of power potential.

Vidich, Arthur J., and Bensman, Joseph. *Small Town in Mass Society* (Princeton, N.J.: Princeton University Press, 1958.)
   Reviews:
      Lenski, Gerhard E., *American Sociological Review* 23 (August 1958) 468-69.
      Bell, Colin, *Sociological Review* 18 (March 1970) 140-42.
   For three years, the authors studied the daily life of "Springdale," a town of 2,500 people in upstate New York. They see Springdale as a homogeneous community in which the maintenance of harmony is a fundamental objective of community leaders. Community decision making is dominated by a small and relatively cohesive coalition of economic and social dominants. The authors illustrate that those with power maintain their influence not   only through their own energy and the skillful exercise of their resources, but by meeting the general needs of the community, at least to the extent that effective opposition to their hegemony cannot be mobilized.
   Emphasis is placed on the impingement of the larger society on the economic and political autonomy of the community. The authors report that because of this impingement, the power of local decision-makers over the life of the community has steadily declined. They observe that stress among leaders and among other residents results from the need to adjust prevailing myths with social reality thrust upon the community by its integration in the mass society.

Walter, Benjamin. "Political Decision Making in Arcadia," in F. Stuart Chapin, Jr., and Shirley F. Weiss, eds., *Urban Growth Dynamics in a Regional Cluster of Cities* (New York: John Wiley and Sons, 1962) pp. 141-87.
   The distribution of political influence in "Arcadia," North Carolina (population 100,000) is identified through an eight- to ten-year study of three key issues in this

community. The issues studied were the development of a new city hall, urban renewal, and public housing. Knowledge, time, and motivation are determined to be major sources of political power.

On the basis of the case studies used, the author concludes that political power in Arcadia is shared by a number of interests and that these interests compete with one another for shares of the community's resources. He notes that the various competing factions are not class based.

Walter, Benjamin. "Political Decision Making in North Carolina Cities," *Prod* 3 (May 1960) 18-21.

In this report on research in progress, the author provides a commentary on the various approaches to the study of decision making. The focus of research is how decisions are made, which the author considers superior to the question of who makes decisions. Rather than rely on after-the-fact interviews to reconstruct decisional processes, the relative influence of individuals at different stages of the decision-making process will be observed by a specially trained researcher. The results of this technique will be compared with those obtained from using the reputational technique. The author concludes with a brief discussion of three types of political systems: 1) the undifferentiated ruling elite, 2) the polynucleated elite, and 3) a countervailing elite system.

Walton, John. "Development Decision Making: A Comparative Study in Latin America," *American Journal of Sociology* 75 (March 1970) 828-51.

This study explores the interrelationship between the structure of power and development decision making in two Latin American areas — Guadalajara in Mexico and Cali in Colombia. Through interviews with positional leaders in the public and private sectors, a group of influentials was selected and subsequently interviewed. Also interviewed were leading participants in decisions related to development suggested by respondents. By a number of standards, the Guadalajara region is more advanced economically than Cali. The author attempts to account for this difference in terms of the social organization and structure of power in the two areas. The findings of the study indicate that decisional activities that promote development are more likely (1) when power is the property of authoritative organizations (or individuals representing them) rather than the property of individuals; (2) when power is broadly distributed, but (3) when the inequality of power among actors is relatively great; (4) when there is greater coordination of power, and (5) when there is a greater amount of total power. The author concludes with some observations about the consequences of development for changes in social power arrangements.

Wildavsky, Aaron B. *Leadership in a Small Town* (Totowa, N.J.: Bedminster Press, 1964).

Reviews:

Bensman, Joseph, *American Journal of Sociology* 70 (January 1965) 483-84.
D'Antonio, William V., *Annals* 363 (January 1966) 199-200.
Kammerer, Gladys M., *Journal of Politics* 27 (May 1965) 439-40.
Kellstadt, Lyman, "Atlanta to Oretown: Identifying Community Elites," *Public Administration Review* 25 (June 1965) 161-68.

Danielson, Michael, *Public Opinion Quarterly* 3 (Fall 1966) 517-18.

This study of Oberlin, Ohio (population 8,000) replicates and extends Robert Dahl's study of New Haven, Connecticut. Wildavsky identifies the structure of influence in Oberlin through a study of every issue of consequence in the community during the period 1957-1961. Persons who were influential in securing favorable decisions in each area (favorable to themselves or to their objectives) were interviewed and asked to suggest the names of others who were involved. Eventually, almost all key participants in the decisions which took place during this time were interviewed. In addition, observers were stationed with key officials in the community to observe the ways issues developed and the ways in which they were disposed. In an attempt to discover if issues of concern to persons of various backgrounds had been suppressed through the exercise of influence, Wildavsky interviewed a random sample of the community citizens to determine those things they would like to see done in the community.

He concludes that patterns of influence in Oberlin are pluralistic, that leaders tend to center about specific issues, and that the persons who hold general influence over a range of issues are those who hold public office. It is also found that local elections are competitive and that political leaders are, at least in general terms, responsive to various interests in the community. Moreover they are conscious of their dependence on the local electorate for continued influence.

Wildavsky also compares his finds to a pattern of influence determined by reputational techniques and concludes that reputation for leadership is an inadequate measure of an individual's actual participation in shaping the outcomes of community policies. The author also draws upon other community studies and formulates general propositions about "why American cities are pluralist."

Williams, Oliver P., and Adrian, Charles. *Four Cities: A Study in Comparative Policy Making* (Philadelphia: University of Pennsylvania Press, 1963).

Reviews:

Pettengill, Dwynal B., *Journal of Politics* 26 (August 1964) 726-27.

Anton, Thomas J., *Midwest Journal of Political Science* 8 (May 1964) 212-15.

Hennessy, Bernard, *Western Political Quarterly* 17 (June 1964) 385-86.

Schulze, Robert O., *American Sociological Review* 29 (August 1964) 609-10.

Jennings, M. Kent, *American Journal of Sociology* 70 (November 1964) 390.

Fagin, Henry, *Annals* 353 (May 1964) 147-48.

Community decision making in four midwestern cities ranging in size from 50,000 to 75,000 is analyzed through past records, newspaper reports, personal observation and the reports of informants. The structure of power in these communities is characterized as more or less pluralistic in each case but with different types of groups holding predominant influence in each community. It is found that the more fragmented power structures are associated with lower average family income, ward rather than at-large elections, and less community-wide consensus concerning the positive role to be played by local government. A typology of local government is developed using community policy-making norms as the criteria for classification.

Wilson, Everett K. "Determinants of Participation in Policy Formation in a College Community," *Human Relations* 7 (August 1954) 287-312.

DISSERTATIONS

Akenson, Curtis Burcette. "Selected Facets of Community Influence on Political Power in the Redevelopment of the Minneapolis Lower Loop," Ph.D., University of Minnesota, 1962. (Order No. 63-1187) m $5.25; x $18.70.

Ashley, Thomas J. "Power and Politics in Community Planning: An Empirical Analysis of Four Selected Policy Decisions Made in Anaheim, California between 1945-1960," Ph.D., Claremont Graduate School and University Center, 1962. (Order No. 63-252) m $3.90; x $13.75.

Barlow, Henry Mikel. "Community Power Structure and Decision Making in an Urban Community," Ph.D., Ohio State University, 1968. (Order No. 69-4841) m $3.00; x $10.15.

Blankenship, Lloyd Vaughn. "Organizational Support and Community Leadership in Two New York State Communities," Ph.D., Cornell University, 1962. (Order No. 63-747) m $3.00; x $8.20.

Bloomberg, Warner. "The Structure of Power in Stackton," Ph.D., University of Chicago, 1960.

Bouma, D. "An Analysis of the Power Position of the Real Estate Board in Grand Rapids, Michigan," Ph.D., Michigan State University, 1952.

Cargan, Leonard. "Community Power in a Dormitory City," Ph.D., Wayne State University, 1968. (Order No. 71-2971) 123 pp.

Carpenter, D.B. "Some Factors Associated with Influence Position in the Associational Structure of a Rural Community," Ph.D., University of Washington, 1951.

Clare, Donald Alan. "Organizational Power: Influence and Control in a Philippine Community Development Organization," Ph.D., University of Oregon, 1965. (Order No. 66-5400) m $3.00; x $9.25.

Clauss, William A. "An Analytical Look at the Black, the White, and the Overall Power Structures of a Selected County in Florida," Ph.D., University of Miami, 1970. (Order No. 71-4318) 250 pp.

Conway, William J. "Power Structures in Two Communities: A Comparative Analysis," Ph.D., Louisiana State University and Agricultural and Mechanical College, 1970. (Order No. 71-6552) 222 pp.

Daniels, Bruce C. "Large Town Power Structures in Eighteenth Century Connecticut: An Analysis of Political Leadership in Hartford, Norwich, and Fairfield," Ph.D., University of Connecticut, 1970. (Order No. 71-15, 972) 247 pp.

D'Antonio, William V. "National Images of Business and Political Elites in Two Border Cities," Ph.D., Michigan State University, 1958.

Drake, George F. "Elites and Voluntary Associations: A Study of Community Power in Manizabes, Colombia," Ph.D., University of Wisconsin, 1970. (Order No. 71-3455) 334 pp.

Duggan, Thomas Joseph. "Aldermanic Campaign Techniques and Decision-Making Systems in Two Communities," Ph.D., University of Illinois, 1963. (Order No. 64-6048) m $3.00; x $7.80.

French, Robert Mills. "Cornucopia in Transition," Ph.D., University of Wisconsin, 1967. (Order No. 67-16, 940) m $3.40; x $11.95.

Gagan, Richard J. "Pluralism and Community Structure: A Comparative Analysis of Rural Centers in New York State," Ph.D., Cornell University, 1969. (Order No. 70-11, 229) m $4.00; x $10.60. 232 pp.

Garvelink, Roger H. "A Study of Citizens Committees: The Relationship of the Positions in the Community Power Structure of the Citizens Serving as Members of Citizens Committees and the Citizens Advocating the Use of Citizens Committees," Ph.D., University of Michigan, 1970. (Order No. 71-15, 157) 181 pp.

Gravel, Pierre Bettez. "The Play for Power: Description of a Community in Eastern Ruanda," Ph.D., University of Michigan, 1962. (Order No. 63-353) m $4.15; x $14.65.

Harper, Joe W. "A Study of Community Power Structure in Certain School Districts in the State of Texas and Its Influence on Bond Elections," Ed.D., North Texas State University, 1965. (Order No. 65-15118) m $3.00; x $9.90.

Hellenga, Robert Dean. "A Study of Professional and Community Leadership Roles as They Are Assumed by Public School Teachers in Selected School Districts in Michigan," Ed.D., Michigan State University, 1963. (Order No. 64-4967) m $3.00; x $8.00.

Holderman, James Bowker. "Decision Making and Community Leadership in the Village of Winnetka, Illinois," Ph.D., Northwestern University, 1962. (Order No. 63-1301) m $3.00; x $9.25.

Hoskin, Gary. "Community Power and Political Modernization: A Study of a Venezuelan City," Ph.D., University of Illinois, Urbana, 1966.

Hudson, James Ryland. "Power with Low Prestige: A Study of Labor Unions in a Dependent Community," Ph.D., University of Michigan, 1965. (Order No. 66-5085) m $4.35; x $15.30.

Jones, Joseph H., Jr. "A Comparative Analysis of Community Leaders and Non-Leaders in a North Central Kentucky Community," Ph.D., University of Kentucky, 1956.

Klein, Henry Louis. "Community Organization Leadership in Philadelphia," Ed.D., Temple University, 1965. (Order No. 65-9489) m $3.00; x $8.40.

Larson, Calvin James. "Economic and Ecological Factors in Relation to Community Leadership Structure: A Comparative and Historical Analysis of Two Oregon Communities," Ph.D., University of Oregon, 1965. (Order No. 66-618) m $3.15; x $11.05.

Light, Kenneth Henry. "Community Power Structures and School District Reorganization," Ed.D., University of Colorado, 1964. (Order No. 65-4257) m $3.15; x $11.05.

Longstreth, J.W. "The Relationship of Beliefs of Community Leaders, Teachers, and Voters to School Fiscal Policy and Typology of Community Power Structure," Ed.D., University of Florida, 1967. (Order No. 68-9500) m $3.00; x $5.60.

Miller, Jack A. "The Effects of the Power Structure upon the Decison-Making Process of Boards of Education in Selected Missouri School Districts," Ed.D., University of Missouri-Columbia, 1970. (Order No. 71-3362) 143 pp.

Nance, Jack Lee. "A Study of the Leadership Role of the Superintendent and High School Principal within Selected Communities of Oklahoma," Ph.D., University of Oklahoma, 1965. (Order No. 65-9753) m $3.00; x $8.20.

Perkins, Larry Manson. "Leadership in a New York Rural Community," D.S.S., Syracuse University, 1963. (Order No. 64-7468) m $3.00; x $10.15.

Powers, Ronald Clair. "Social Power in a Rural Community," Ph.D., Iowa State University of Science and Technology, 1963. (Order No. 63-7267) m $3.00; x $8.00.

Rhyne, E. H. "Party Politics and the Decision-Making Process: A Study at the County Level," Ph.D., University of North Carolina, 1957.

Rogers, Robert Burtch. "Perception of the Power Structure by Social Class in a California Community," Ph.D., University of Southern California, 1962. (Order No. 62-6083) m $3.45; x $12.15.

Roth, Marian Ilene. "Unification and Community Values in a Metropolitan Region," Ph.D., University of Iowa, 1969. (Order No. 69-13, 174) m $3.00; x $7.40.

Scaggs, James Lewis. "Interaction Patterns of Superintendents with Community Power Systems in Twenty-four Selected School Districts," Ed. D., University of Florida, 1968. (Order No. 69-17, 039) m $3.00; x $10.15.

Schneider, Herbert H. "A Comparative Study of Political Power and Educational Decision Making in Two Small City School Districts," Ph.D., Ohio State University, 1969. (Order No. 70-6875) m $3.20; x $11.05. 245 pp.

Schulze, Robert O. "Economic Dominance and Public Leadership: A Study of the Structure and Process of Power in an Urban Community," Ph.D., University of Michigan, 1956.

Seeker, William A. "Power Structure and School Bond Elections," Ph.D., Texas A. & M. University, 1969. (Order No. 70-11, 580) m $4.00; x $8.60. 188 pp.

Simpson, Dick Weldon. "The Political Evolution of Two African Towns," Ph.D., Indiana University, 1968. (Order No. 69-7116) m $3.30; x $11.50.

Stone, Clarence Nathan. "The City Manager and Community Power: Leadership and Policy Making in a Council-Manager City," Ph.D., Duke University, 1963. (Order No. 63-4249) m $3.30; x $11.50.

Swanson, Bert E. "Power and Politics: A Community Formulates Electric Power Policy," Ph.D., University of Oregon, 1959.

Tait, John L. "Power Structures by Issue Area in Five Iowa Communities," Ph.D., Iowa State University, 1970. (Order No. 70-25, 829) m $4.00; x $7.60. 165 pp.

Vanderbok, William G. "Decisions and Nondecisions: Elite Structures and Political Power in an Indiana City," Ph.D., Indiana University, 1969. (Order No. 70-10, 277) m $4.55; x $16.00. 355 pp.

Van Der Merwe, Hendrik Willem. "Leadership in a Saskatchewan Community: The Impact of Industrialization," Ph.D., University of California, Los Angeles, 1963. (Order No. 63-6842) m $3.00; x $8.40.

Vannan, Donald Antrim. "Methods of Identifying Community Power Structures Utilized by Chief School Administrators in Selected School Districts of Pennsylvania," Ed.D., Pennsylvania State University, 1962. (Order No. 63-3092) m $3.00; x $6.00.

Vinton, Dennis A. "The Relationship between the Power Structure and Parks and Recreation in a Large Urban Community," Re.D., Indiana University, 1969. (Order No. 70-1704) m $4.00; x $8.60. 188 pp.

Warren, Elizabeth A. C. "The Anatomy of Decision Making in a Local Community: A Study of Kansas City," Ph.D., University of Nebraska, 1970. (Order No. 71-3663) 253 pp.

Whitten, Norman E., Jr. "An Analysis of Social Structure and Change: Profile of a Northwest Ecuadorian Town," Ph.D., University of North Carolina, 1964.

Chapter 3

THE METHODOLOGY OF COMMUNITY POWER RESEARCH

Abu-Laban, Baha. "Leader Visibility in a Local Community," *Pacific Sociological Review* 4 (Fall 1961) 73-78.

Using data from his study of "Pacific Town," Washington (population 5,000), the author compares the perception of community leaders on the part of a panel of "knowledgeables" and a random sample of the town residents. He finds that residents who have a high degree of social participation, are of higher class, male, and have longer periods of residence in the community, are: (1) more likely to nominate leaders than are residents who do not have these characteristics and (2) are more likely to nominate the same leaders nominated by the "knowledgeables." The author concludes that leader visibility is a function of the attributed leader's overt involvement in the community, his social class, his personality traits, and the publicity he has received.

Abu-Laban, Baha. "The Reputational Approach in the Study of Community Power: A Critical Evaluation," *Pacific Sociological Review* 8 (Spring 1965) 35-42.

The various components of the reputational approach to the study of community power are discussed and the criticisms of that approach are examined. The author discusses the assumptions upon which the reputational approach is based and argues that the approach has substantial usefulness.

Abu-Laban, Baha. "Self Conception and Appraisal by Other: A Study of Community Leaders," *Sociology and Social Research* 48 (October 1963) 32-37.

This article examines the relationship between perception of influence by a community's residents and self-conceptions of community leaders. The site of the study is "Pacific Town," Washington (population 5,000). The twenty-five leaders who made up the leadership group were identified by reputational techniques. Then the attitudes of citizens were taken from a random sample of sixty-eight community residents. The results of the study were that the residents' appraisals of community leaders were related to the latter's: (a) self-conceptions of perceived influence; (b) self-conceptions of perceived instrumentality; (c) self-conceptions of perceived belongingness in a leadership group; (d) self-conceptions of perceived efficacy of their leadership; and (e) self-conceptions of perceived community support.

Agger, Robert E. "Panel Studies of Comparative Political Decision Making: The Dynamics of Urban Renewal," in M. Kent Jennings and L. Harmon Ziegler, eds., *The Electoral Process* (Englewood Cliffs, N.J.: Prentice-Hall, 1966) pp. 265-89.

The author argues that the potential of panel studies for studying community politics on a systematic comparative basis is substantially untapped by analysts of local government. He describes the use of the panel study for the analysis of various aspects of decision making regarding urban renewal programs in two Oregon cities.

Agger, Robert E. "Power Attributions in the Local Community: Theoretical and Research Considerations," *Social Forces* 34 (May 1956) 322-31.

A random sample of 260 adults in a city near Eugene, Oregon (population of about 2,000) was asked to nominate community leaders. Half of the sample were not political participants and 21 percent could name no one as being generally influential. On the other hand, when asked to nominate persons influential in specific areas (such as school issues, government issues, etc.) the interviewees were usually able to make nominations. The author suggests that a reputation for general leadership may result from the tendency of respondents to transfer perceptions of specialized influence when asked to identify persons who are generally influential.

The author does not claim that the distribution of influence identified by his respondents represents the community power structure but suggests that this approach is a useful way of beginning the search for community power. A rather broad distribution of influence centered around specific issue areas was found. It is also noted that formal organizations and certain "advisors" (persons from whom citizens would seek advice) acted as channels of communication between community leaders and the rest of the citizenry.

Aiken, Michael, and Alford, Robert. "Community Structure and Innovation: The Case of Public Housing," *American Political Science Review* 64 (September 1970) 843-64.

Five theories of community innovation are employed to explain the differing responses of communities to the creation of a public housing program. The theories deal with political culture, centralization of formal political structure, community differentiation and continuity, community integration, and the concentration or diffusion of community power. Although the focus of the article is public policy, the authors pose several relevant questions about theoretical assumptions and concepts central to the study of community power. The theory drawn from the literature put simply is that the fewer the actors, whether citizen or elite, the more concentrated the power, and, the more likely is innovation in public policy.

Although the authors find in their empirical analysis that cities with characteristics associated with diffusion of power — high MPO ratio, high educational level, high percentage middle class — have less public housing, as the theory predicts, they also find that middle-class characteristics are associated with more centralized power arrangements (i.e., fewer active power groups and actors), which contradicts the basic assumption underlying the theory. The authors are unable to explain the inconsistency, but their findings point up different usages of the concept of concentration or centralization of power, and raise questions about the concept's meaning.

Aiken, Michael, and Alford, Robert R. "Community Structure and Innovation: The Case of Urban Renewal," *American Sociological Review* 35 (August 1970) 650-55.

An examination of the same cities and variables with the dependent variable in this case being the nature of the community urban renewal program.

Arensberg, Conrad M. "The Community Study Method," *American Journal of Sociology* 60 (September 1954) 109-24.

The historical background of sociologists' interests in the study of community is examined. The origins of the various methodologies utilized by these researchers are also discussed. The author argues that most methods are inadequate because they focus on isolated problems and deal with them abstractly. He suggests that problems be studied in terms of their interrelationships and their relation to the entire community context. He views the community as a laboratory for examining social and psychological interconnections.

Bachrach, Peter, and Baratz, Morton S. "Decisions and Non-Decisions: An Analytical Framework," *American Political Science Review* 57 (September 1963) 632-42.

It is argued that force, influence, or authority — as these terms are most popularly understood — are not the only, and may not be even the major factor underlying the process of decision making. The authors regard "non-decision making" as a positive phenomenon which prevents certain grievances from becoming issues which call for decisions. The "non-decision-making process" involves the impact of the mobilization of bias upon a latent issue and it involves anticipation, adjustment, and accommodation on the part of those who have power in order to avoid confrontation. The authors argue that the "non-decision-making process" is subject to analysis. An attempt is made to distinguish between such terms as force and power and influence and authority.

Bachrach, Peter, and Baratz, Morton S. "The Two Faces of Power," *American Political Science Review* 56 (December 1962) 947-52.

The authors argue that while sociologists, for the most part, have failed to establish empirically the nature of community power, political scientists have seen only one aspect of that phenomenon. They level their criticism at the "pluralist approach" to the study of community power used by political scientists and specifically at Robert Dahl's study of New Haven, Connecticut. They argue that "pluralists" have failed to establish criteria by which to distinguish between relatively unimportant and critical community decisions. They suggest the latter might be those decisions which change the "rules of the game" of community decision making in terms of the types of issues dealt with and the manner in which those issues are resolved. Secondly, they argue that attention cannot be confined to the overt process of decision making on specific issues but should also be concerned with determining whether or not the matters which are dealt with are defined and restricted by community elites to those matters which the elites consider to be "safe."

Baltzell, E.D. "Elite and Upper Class Indexes in Metropolitan America," in R. Bendix and S. Lipset, eds., *Class, Status and Power* (Glencoe, Illinois: The Free Press, 1953).

Barth, Ernest A.T., and Johnson, Stuart D. "Community Power and a Typology of Social Issues," *Social Forces* 38 (October 1959) 29-32.

The authors seek to formulate a multidimensional scheme for classifying issues which will be related to alternative patterns of community power. They speculate on the relationship between different types of issues, different types of leaders and different patterns of decision making. The five dimensions in the typology are: (1) unique-recurrent, (2) salient-nonsalient to leadership, (3) salient-nonsalient to community publics; (4) effective action possible-effective action impossible and (5) local-cosmopolitan.

Bassett, Raymond E. "Sampling Problems in Influence Studies," *Sociometry* 12 (November 1948) 320-28.

Blackwell, Gordon W. "Community Analysis," in Roland Young, ed., *Approaches to the Study of Politics* (Evanston, Illinois: Northwestern University Press, 1958) pp. 305-17.

Various ways in which the term "community" is conceptualized by sociologists are discussed. These conceptualizations are placed in historical perspective and are related to different methods and approaches which sociologists have used in the analysis of communities. He notes that studies have tended to move in scope from macroscopic to microscopic, from concern for static situations to concern for processes, and from normative to analytical modes of inquiry.

Blackwell, Gordon W. "A Theoretical Framework for Sociological Research in Community Organization," *Social Forces* 33 (October 1954) 57-64.

Following Parsons, the author suggests that communities can be considered as a set of dynamic interacting social systems. He explains some of the ways in which analysis of those systems can be operationalized and emphasizes the importance of examining the roles and the ecology which define and shape the structure of the community. Social organization is seen as a means by which community identification and togetherness is secured. Social organization proceeds spontaneously while community development is a nationally directed process. The implications of this distinction are examined. The author also suggests a number of hypotheses which could form the basis for future research.

Blankenship, L. Vaughn. "Community Power and Decision Making: A Comparative Evaluation of Measurement Techniques," *Social Forces* 43 (December 1964) 207-16.

It is noted that a major criticism of the reputational approach to the study of community power is that the method ordains the results. The author argues, on the other hand, that by confining themselves to analyses of decisions in which the formal organs of local government were involved, political scientists have equated community power with public, i.e., governmental, power. He argues that both the reputational approach and the decision-making approach have something to offer and that each technique tends to provide access to a somewhat different set of elites. He illustrates the utility of using both approaches in a comparative study of two New York communities and demonstrates considerable overlap in the results derived from each method. (For a more extensive commentary of the study of these two communities, see the note above on Robert Presthus' *Man at the Top*, 1964.)

Booth, David A., and Adrian, Charles R. "Simplifying the Discovery of Elites," *American Behavioral Scientist* (October 1961) 14-16.

Utilizing data collected by Smuckler and Belknap in their study of "Community A," the authors compare the nominations of community leaders which have been obtained from fifty-six informants with a list of leaders nominated by only fourteen of those fifty-six informants selected on the basis of the Miller-Form technique. The Miller-Form approach to the identification of community leaders relies upon nominations provided by two "knowledgeables" in each of seven sectors of the community. It was found that the "Miller-Form panel" yielded almost as many leadership nominations. Perhaps more important, it yielded a list of fifteen top influentials, all of whom were included in the list of seventeen top influentials who had been selected on the basis of the fifty-six informants' nominations. Moreover, the ranking of the "most influential" was very similar, using the two different approaches. It is concluded that the Miller-Form technique is an economical and accurate method of formulating a list of persons with a reputation for community leadership.

Curtis, James E., and Petras, John W. "Community Power, Power Studies and the Sociology of Knowledge," *Human Organization* 29 (Fall 1970) 204-18.

This article surveys the methods and findings of eighty-three studies on the power structure in particular communities — all of such studies published between 1950 and 1968. Articles were analyzed and coded for (1) disciplinary background of the author(s), (2) method of inquiry — reputational, decisional, case study or combined, and (3) type of power structure found — pyramidal, factional, coalitional or amorphous. It was found that disciplinary background influences the type of method used; thirty-four out of fifty sociology studies employed the reputational technique whereas fifteen of twenty-two political scientists used the decisional approach alone or in combination with the reputational. Furthermore, the reputational approach tends to identify pyramidal structures, whereas the decisional approach seems to discover more pluralist coalitional structures. As a result, political scientists have tended to find pluralist power structures whereas sociologists have been more likely to uncover elite control. The authors relate their findings to a discussion of the sociology of knowledge. An appendix is provided which lists all the studies analyzed including the codes for method and findings.

Dahl, Robert A. "A Critique of the Ruling Elite Model," *American Political Science Review* 52 (June 1958) 463-69.

The author argues that the "ruling elite model" assumes the existence of important characteristics of political and social systems without empirical backing. He suggests a number of ways to test the theory implicit in the ruling elite model in terms of research requirements and he asserts that these requirements have never been fulfilled. He concludes by discussing possible objections to the criteria he advances as necessary and sufficient to establish empirically the identity of those who rule a given political system.

Dahl, Robert A. "The Analysis of Influence in Local Communities" in Charles Adrian, ed., *Social Science in Community Action* (East Lansing: Institute for Community Development, Michigan State University, 1961) pp. 25-42.

Dahl says that the way in which community decisions may be reached can take many forms. In order to identify community leadership, one should examine specific sets of decisions relating to certain issues, which Dahl calls issue scopes. He suggests that in most urban communities, there will be a number of issue scopes and that leader influential in one issue scope will not be influential in another. The basic task in establishing the nature of influence in local communities is to establish the "distribution of influence," that is, the number of people who exercise influence and the amounts of influence they enjoy. It must also be determined whether leaders prevail in the face of opposition or because no one is contesting a specific decision outcome.

D'Antonio, William V., and Erickson, Eugene C. "The Reputational Technique as a Measure of Community Power: An Evaluation Based on Comparative and Longitudinal Studies," *American Sociological Review* 27 (June 1962) 362-76.

In response to several criticisms of the reputational approach to the study of community power, the authors seek to establish its validity by comparing the results of studies made between 1954 and 1959 in communities along the southwestern border of the United States. They found that in no community did key influentials exercise power over all issues. On the other hand, they found that some of those to whom substantial general influence had been attributed ("key influentials") played a role in each of one or more specific issue areas within the six communities studied. Those who were considered the most influential in specific areas were also usually considered to be among the most influential generally.

The results of the findings of two communities which were studied during a five-year period indicated that the general pattern of leadership found in the earlier research prevailed in the later research. The authors conclude that this finding suggests that the reputational approach is reliable over time. While the authors conclude that there is evidence of a relationship between attributed influence and the actual exercise of power, actual participation in the resolution of specific issues in each community is not discussed.

D'Antonio, William V.; Ehrlich, Howard J.; and Erickson, Eugene C. "Further Notes on the Study of Community Power," *American Sociological Review* 27 (December 1962) 848-53.

In response to specific criticisms by Raymond Wolfinger and Nelson Polsby of the authors' earlier defense of the reputational approach to the study of community power, the authors seek to counter the attacks on the reputational approach and to further explicate their specific justifications of that approach. In short, this article is a rejoinder to articles by Polsby and Wolfinger in the same edition of *American Sociological Review.*

Danzger, M. Herbert. "Community Power Structure Problems and Continuities," *American Sociological Review* 29 (October 1964) 707-17.

The reputational and decisional approaches to the study of community power are examined and both are criticized. It is suggested that the criticisms of the reputational approach are matters subject to empirical inquiry.

It is stressed that some of the difficulties involved in the study of community power have to do with the problem of defining power. The author suggests that power might be considered the potentiality for action. The three major variables involved in the measurement of potential power are: (1) the number of "lines of action" each potential actor sees open to affecting a given decision; (2) the resources the individual has appropriate to the decisions which he sees as open to him; and (3) the desire the individual has to affect the outcome of the decision.

Davis, Morris, and Weinbaum, Marvin G. *Metropolitan Decision Processes: An Examination of Case Studies,* American Politics Research Series (Chicago: Rand McNally and Co., 1969).

The authors examine the process of decision making for issues that take place in and are of importance to major American cities. The findings are derived from interactions reported in 32 case studies of community decisions, selected from the existing literature. In the final chapter, the authors explore the ways that process analysis can be applied to the study of the distribution of power in the community, as well as other theoretical concerns among students of community politics. They set forth a series of hypotheses about the decision-making process derived from the literature on community power.

Dick, Harry. "A Method for Ranking Community Influentials," *American Sociological Review* 25 (June 1960) 395-99.

Eight lawyers are provided with a list of ninety-seven persons and invited to rank these persons on a five-point scale of influence. It is found that the influence each attributes to the various persons listed is relatively consistent with that of the listings furnished by the group as a whole. It is concluded, therefore, that the reputational approach to the study of community power is valid in the sense that the nominations of leadership given by representatives of a given institutional sector are not heavily influenced by the personal characteristics and experience of the rater.

Downes, Bryan T. "Municipal Social Rank and Characteristics of Local Political Leaders," *Midwest Journal of Political Science* 12 (November 1968) 514-37.

The hypothesis that the municipal context within which local political leaders function may in part determine, on the one hand, their background characteristics, and, on the other, their role perceptions and policy attitudes, has been tested using city councilmen in thirty-seven suburban municipalities in St. Louis County. Context, measured by a composite index derived from data on median family income, median value of owner-occupied dwellings, and proportion of persons employed in professional occupations, was related to characteristics of suburban city councilmen. Contrary to expectations, municipal social rank had only a limited effect on the role perceptions and policy attitudes of these elected officials; local political leaders, despite variations in context, exhibited very similar representational role perceptions and policy attitudes. A strong positive relationship was found, however, between a municipality's social rank and the socioeconomic status and voting behavior of its councilmen.

Ehle, Emily. "Techniques for Study of Leadership," *Public Opinion Quarterly* 13 (Summer 1949) 235-40.

Ehrlich, Howard J. "The Reputational Approach to the Study of Community Power," *American Sociological Review* 26 (December 1961) 926-27.

The author argues that while reputation for community power may not be the same thing as actual community power, it is nevertheless a phenomenon worth studying. He concludes that, "If we can ascertain that the way in which people perceive the power structure of a local political system affects the way in which they behave toward that system then surely we are dealing with a very meaningful, indeed very useful, consideration."

Ehrlich, Howard J. "The Social Psychology of Reputations for Community Leadership," *Sociological Quarterly* 8 (Fall 1967) 514-30.

It is suggested that despite all the commentary on the validity of the reputational approach to the study of community power, the social-psychological dimensions of the reputational procedure have been largely ignored. Based on data collected by the National Opinion Research Center from a sample of 1,277 county residents of Prince George's County, Maryland (population 425,000), the author describes the socioeconomic characteristics of community involvement and the participatory behavior of persons who are and are not proficient in nominating community leaders. He concludes that there is an inherent bias to the reputational approach. Using community "knowledgeables" as a panel of judges tends to overstate the influence and the involvement in community affairs of persons of relatively high socioeconomic status. He illustrates, moreover, that this bias is more serious in the case of the so-called two-step approach to assessment of community influentials than in the seemingly less sophisticated approach of using the one-step approach. The author concludes with a substantive appendix which codifies the major statements in the research literature on the social psychology of leader reputations.

Ehrlich, Howard J., and Bauer, Mary Lou. "Newspaper Citation and Reputation for Community Leadership," *American Sociological Review* 30 (June 1965) 411-15.

The authors demonstrate that community leaders appear with considerable frequency in the local press and that this appearance seems to contribute to their reputation for leadership. In the community studies, political office holders were more likely to be cited in the newspapers than others who were reputed to have power. The authors point to the need to draw the distinction between the power of a person which adheres to his position and the power he has that transcends the particular office or position he holds.

Fanelli, A.A. "A Typology of Community Leadership Based on Influence and Interaction within the Leader Sub-system," *Social Forces* 34 (May 1956) 332-38.

Form, William H. "Labor and Community Influentials: A Comparative Study of Participation and Imagery," *Industrial and Labor Relations Review* 17 (October 1963) 3-19.

Foskett, John M. and Hohle, Raymond. "Measurement of Influence in Community Affairs," Proceedings of Pacific Sociological Society published in *Research Studies of the State College of Washington* 25 (June 1957) 148-54.

Fox, Douglas M. "The Identification of Community Leaders by the Reputational and Decisional Methods: Three Case Studies and an Empirical Analysis of the Literature," *Sociology and Social Research* 54 (October 1969) 94-103.
The author analyzes methods of identifying leaders by comparing the findings resulting from use of the reputational and decisional approaches in three small (13,000 to 17,000 population) New England towns – communities "C", "D", and "E". Five decisions were studied in each of the first two communities, and three in the last. Decisional participants served as the nomination panel for reputational leaders. He compares the results with those of other writers who have employed both methods, and, in particular, with the work of James D. Preston ("Identification of Community Leaders," *Sociology and Social Research* 53 [January 1969] 204-16), who concluded that in small and medium-sized towns, these two approaches, as well as the positional, will produce the same results. Fox, on the basis of his case studies, rejects this assertion. After examining all studies in which the two methods were used jointly, however, he points out that although different approaches reveal different groupings of leaders, the two methods do not lead "to the discovery of different types of structures of power."

Freeman, Linton C.; Fararo, Thomas J.; Bloomberg, Warner, Jr.; and Sunshine, Morris C. "Locating Leaders in Local Communities: A Comparison of Some Alternative Approaches," *American Sociological Review* 28 (October 1963) 791-98.
This study of participation in the decision-making process in Syracuse tests the extent to which four techniques for identifying leaders reveal the same group of leaders. These techniques are based on the following criteria for identifying leaders: (1) those who participate in decision making, (2) those who hold formal positions of authority, (3) those who are reputed to be leaders, and (4) those who are highly active in voluntary organizations. The method employed in this study was to

identify a large number of important community issues and then to interview all those who were involved in the resolution of each issue because of their formal position or their participation. In all, 550 participants in thirty-nine issues were interviewed. Among respondents, separate lists were created of the most active participants in decision making, the most active organizational members, the most highly reputed leaders, and the heads of the most important organizations in business, government, the professions, etc. When the four sets were compared, there was little agreement in determining leaders except between reputation and position. The authors conclude that different techniques reveal different basic types of "leaders." First, there are the "institutional leaders" who hold important positions and are reputed to be influential but do not participate extensively in decision making. Second, the "effectors" are the workers in the actual process of decision making who are located by studying participation. Third, there are the "activists" who are highly active in voluntary organizations and have an impact on community affairs due to their large commitment of time and effort.

French, Robert Mills, and Aiken, Michael. "Community Power in Cornucopia: A Replication of the Bonjean Technique of Identifying Community Leaders," *Sociological Quarterly* 9 (Spring 1968) 261-70.

The purpose of this study is to replicate the Bonjean technique for identifying leaders in a much smaller city — "Cornucopia" in Illinois had a population of 11,220 in 1960 — than the two communities studied previously by Bonjean and by Miller and Dirksen (in an earlier replication). The findings are quite similar to the earlier studies. The technique is designed to distinguish among visible, symbolic and concealed leaders. In this study the choices of community leaders by the top men in the reputational study differed significantly from the choices made by lower-ranked reputational leaders.

French, Robert Mills. "Effectiveness of the Various Techniques Employed in the Study of Community Power," *The Journal of Politics* 31 (August 1969) 818-20.

In order to obtain a complete picture of community power in Cornucopia (population 11,220) and to analyze methods of identifying leaders, the author applies the three major techniques. The reputational leaders were identified by a panel composed of the heads of all voluntary organizations. Individuals were designated positional leaders if they (1) held a public office, (2) were civic leaders who held an office in an important voluntary organization, or (3) were economically dominant. The decisional leaders were those who had participated in making decisions which involved large sums of public funds, concerned many participants, or were controversial. The research found almost complete overlap in leaders revealed by the reputational and positional techniques. Slightly more than one-third of the decisional leaders, however, were not included in the list obtained from the reputational approach. When the positional leaders were included, the number not covered dropped to 15 percent (four of twenty-six.) Of the four not revealed by either of the other techniques, only one had an important role in the decisions and none was a key participant. Used alone, the reputational located the *key* participants in every issue and all but two of the important participants. "Thus the substantially different leadership structure supposedly revealed by the decisional techniques was not found in Cornucopia, and the reputational technique did not distort reality." This technique, the author concluded, was very effective for locating leaders, and the most effective for estimating the relative influence of individual leaders. In this case, the decisional technique revealed only lower-ranking participants beyond those discovered by other methods.

Gamson, William A. "Reputation and Resources in Community Politics," *American Journal of Sociology* 72 (September 1966) 121-31.

Fifty-four issues in eighteen New England communities were studied to determine whether those reputed to have political influence in the area were on the winning side of the issue. The communities ranged in population from 2,000 to 100,000; the average was 10,000 residents. Once having identified the issues, the author interviewed those who were reputed to possess political influence. He found little evidence that these leaders were united on many issues. In only three of the communities studied did those who participated in the decision-making process resemble anything like a well-integrated political clique. Thus, this evidence discourages the view that reputational leaders are a cohesive group possessing common objectives.

Persons with a reputation for leadership were on the winning side of an issue three-fourths of the time, even though they were on the most active side of the issue only 56 percent of the time. The author found that those supporting change have very little success in securing that change without the support of at least some reputational leaders. It is concluded that reputation must be viewed as a resource as well as an indicator of resources. His data suggests that those with a reputation for political influence are more often than not actually influential.

Goldhammer, Keith. "Community Power Structure and School Board Membership," *American School Board Journal* 130 (March 1955) 23-25.

Haer, John L. "Social Stratification in Relation to Attitudes Toward Sources of Power in a Community," *Social Forces* 35 (December 1956) 137-42.

A sample of 320 adults in Tallahassee, Florida (population 38,000), were surveyed concerning their attitudes toward various sources of community power (such as service clubs, state offices, courts and businesses). Respondents with the highest socioeconomic status were more likely to hold their views more strongly and were more likely to express more positive attitudes. Those with the lowest socioeconomic status expressed more negative attitudes toward the power sources. The author notes that the nature of the socioeconomic base of Tallahassee, which is the seat of two universities and the state capitol, limits the generalized ability of the findings.

Hanson, Robert C., and Associates. "Predicting a Community Decision: A Test of the Miller-Form Theory," *American Sociological Review* 24 (October 1959) 662-71.

A panel of thirty-six informants representing twelve areas of community affairs was asked to identify: (1) influential groups within their area; (2) the relationship between these groups; and (3) the salience to community groups of two issues coming to a vote in the city of Denver. The data collected thereby is used to test the hypothesis that the outcome of a community issue can be predicted by: (1) determining the critically activated parts of the institutional power structure which are involved for or against a given issue; (2) determining how active and how salient the issue is to these groups; (3) determining the power arrangement of the community power complex; and (4) determining the solidarity and activity of top influentials. The author is able, on the basis of this analysis, to successfully predict with substantial accuracy, the outcome of the votes on a right-to-work amendment to the city charter and a measure to change the civil service procedures.

Hay, Donald G., and Ensminger, Douglas. "Leader-Follower Patterns in Selected Maine Towns," *Rural Sociology* 14 (June 1949) 160-63.

Hill, M.C., and Whiting, Ann. "Some Theoretical and Methodological Problems in Community Studies," *Social Forces* 29 (December 1950) 117-24.

Hunter, Floyd. "Studying Associations and Organizational Structure," in Roland Young, ed., *Approaches to the Study of Politics* (Evanston, Illinois: North-western University Press, 1958) pp. 343-63.
Rather than viewing the community as a series of broad-scale institutions, or as a system of stratification, the author urges that community researchers focus their attention on the interaction among associations and formal organizations and the relative status of such entities. Researchers, he says, should examine the way in which these groups react to specific projects although he notes that many actions of the community power structure (i.e., those groups which enjoy the greatest influence), are often too diffuse to be seen. It is also emphasized that more research needs to be devoted to the examination of intercommunity links, especially the relationship between local communities and the national political and social system. With the help of a panel of "knowledgeables," Hunter identified the 106 most powerful associations in the United States. Through use of mail questionnaires and personal interviews, he sought to determine who the persons most active in these associations viewed as the most powerful groups in the country. Among the conclusions he reaches is that these national associations in many cases have local chapters or affiliates which provide links between the policies developed at the national level and organizations active in the local community.

Janes, Robert W. "A Technique for Describing Community Structure through Newspaper Analysis," *Social Forces* 37 (December 1958) 102-109.

Jennings, M. Kent. "Study of Community Decision-Making," in Bert E. Swanson, ed., *Current Trends in Comparative Community Studies* (Kansas City: Community Studies, Inc., 1962) pp. 18-30.
The author reviews the advantages and disadvantages of four different approaches to understanding the quality of life in American communities. The four orientations examined are: (1) traditional political science; (2) traditional sociology; (3) case studies of issues; and (4) studies of the power structure. He concludes that the last approach, when at its best, utilizes elements of the first three and offers the greatest promise of providing us with an overall understanding of the nature and consequences of political and social decision making.

Jonassen, Christen. "Functional Unities in 88 Community Systems," *American Sociological Review* 26 (June 1961) 399-407.

The author notes that one of the major problems in studying communities is the enormous number of variables with which researchers must deal. In an effort to deal with this problem, the author performs a factor analysis on eighty-two social, economic and demographic variables in eighty-eight counties in Ohio. Seven more or less independent factors are identified: (1) urbanism; (2) welfare (the absence of social and economic pathology); (3) influx (economic and demographic growth); (4) poverty; (5) magnacomplexity (industrialization and commercialism); (6) educational efforts; and (7) proletarianism (characteristics of low-skilled elements of the working force). It is noted that there is some overlap among these seven factors.

Kadushin, Charles. "Power Influence and Social Circles: A New Methodology for Studying Opinion Makers," *American Sociological Review* 33 (October 1968) 685-99.

Problems of identifying elites are rooted in part in barriers to appropriately defined power and elites. Methodologies which focus on reputation, position, or participation in decision making each fail to develop fully the extent to which power elites are interconnected. The author suggests that the concept of social circle, the informal mechanism which links power persons and powerful organizations, serves to locate most of the important issues in the study of elites and serves to unify and formalize methods of locating them. Specifically a snowball sampling technique which begins with persons who hold formal positions in the decision-making process but which employs a broad range of sociometric questions to discover different dimensions of interrelationships should be employed. Once a sample is thus obtained, the elite degree of power or influence should be checked according to reports of what they say they actually do.

Kimball, Solon T., and Pearsall, Marion. "Event Analysis as an Approach to Community Studies," *Social Forces* 34 (October 1955) 58-63.

The authors argue that the approaches to the study of communities utilized by anthropologists and some sociologists have ignored the dynamic aspects of community politics and have, therefore, failed to provide an understanding of the nature and processes of social change. They argue that one way to permit the production or inducement of change is to examine the way in which the community deals with specific and critical events. An example of the utility of this approach is illustrated by reporting on the formulation and implementation of a community health survey in Talladega, Alabama (population 13,000). It is concluded that a core of leaders of formal community institutions dominated the dynamic aspects of decision making in Talladega.

Kornhauser, Ruth R. "The Warner Approach to Stratification," in Reinhard Bendix and Seymour M. Lipset, eds., *Class, Status and Power: A Social Stratification in Comparative Perspective* (New York: The Free Press, 1966) pp. 224-25.

The author describes the research methods utilized by Warner in the conduct of his studies of American communities. She questions the validity of Warner's conclusions on grounds that the way in which he defined the problem in effect preordained the results. Specifically, she argues that Warner's definition of social class is insufficiently broad and objective, that he ignored the consequences of population flux, and that his criteria for allocating persons to different status strata relied too heavily on the values of upper-status persons. She also observes that the types of communities Warner used as laboratories were small and well-integrated and therefore atypical of a very large number of American communities.

Laskin, Richard, and Phillett, Serina. "An Integrative Analysis of Voluntary Associational Leadership and Reputational Influence," *Sociological Inquiry* 35 (Spring 1965) 176-85.

Long, Norton E. "Aristotle and the Study of Local Government," *Social Research* 24 (Autumn 1957) 287-310.

The author criticizes what he perceives to be the narrow approach that political scientists have taken to the study of local government. He suggests that a reorientation might follow the guidelines set forth by Aristotle in his conceptualization of politics and the state as the means to the attainment of ethical values. Long argues that the analysis of political and social stratification, the way in which citizenship is defined and utilized, and the processes by which change occurs, may reveal more about the nature of community politics than will the study of its formal political institutions.

Miller, Delbert C. "The Prediction of Issue Outcome in Community Decision Making," Proceedings of the Pacific Sociological Society published in *Research Studies of the State College of Washington* 25 (June 1957) 137-47.

The outcome of community decision making is seen as resulting from the interrelationship of three factors: (1) those sectors of the community power structure or complex which are activated on a given issue; (2) the alignment of these various sectors on either side of the issue, unstructured, semistructured, or a unified coalition; and (3) the degree of cohesion of the top influentials concerned about the issue. The author develops a formula for operationalizing this hypothesis and for assigning weights to various aspects of his formula. The method used for identifying the community influentials is nomination by a panel of "knowledgeables" in sectors of the community which might be involved with the issue in question. Miller tests his hypothesis on the resolution of a right-to-work proposal which was submitted to the voters in Seattle, Washington in 1956. He reports that he was able to predict the actual vote with great accuracy.

Mulford, Charles L. "On Role Consensus About Community Leaders," *Sociological Inquiry* 36 (Winter 1966) 15-18.

Random samples of 134 rural residents and 195 persons from a city of 15,000, and 36 persons who were considered to be influential in "Western County," Iowa, were interviewed. Each group was asked to specify the obligations and responsibilities of community leaders and to rank these on a five-point scale in terms of their importance. A comparison of the rankings by each of the three groups showed remarkable consensus (virtually unanimity) on the nature of desirable leadership roles and the relative importance attributed to each of those roles.

Ottenberg, Simon. "Leadership and Change in a Coastal Georgia Negro Community," *Phylon* 20 (First Quarter 1959) 7-18.

Parenton, V.J., and Pellegrin, R.J. "Social Structure and the Leadership Factor in a Negro Community in South Louisiana," *Phylon* 17 (March 1956) 74-78.

Polsby, Nelson W. *Community Power and Political Theory* (New Haven: Yale University Press, 1963).

Reviews:

Scoble, Harry M., *Administrative Science Quarterly* 9 (December 1964) 313-15.

D'Antonio, William V., *Social Forces* 42 (March 1964) 375-76.

LaPalombara, Joseph, *Annals* 355 (September 1964) 171-72.

Jennings, M. Kent, *Journal of Politics* 26 (November 1964) 939-40.

Anton, Thomas J., *Midwest Journal of Political Science* 8 (May 1964) 212-15.

Cutright, Phillips, *American Sociological Review* 29 (April 1964) 298-99.

Bloomberg, Warner, Jr., *American Journal of Sociology* 70 (July 1964) 102.

The author critically examines the assumptions and methodology utilized in eight major studies of community influence in which the authors concluded that the nature of social influence was highly stratified and that political and social power rested in the hands of a few socioeconomic elites. Polsby argued that the evidence presented in these "stratification studies" often does not support the conclusions reached by the researchers. He offers a theoretical alternative to the view that a cohesive economic elite dominates most American communities. He also specifies the research methods and empirical criteria which are necessary to determine the structure of influence in a community. The proposed theory and methodology are compared to those research techniques developed and the results thereof in a study of New Haven politics in which the author, Robert Dahl and Raymond Wolfinger participated.

Polsby, Nelson W. "Community Power: Some Reflections on the Recent Literature," *American Sociological Review* 27 (December 1962) 838-41.

This article is a rebuttal to an earlier article by William D'Antonio and Eugene C. Ericksen in which these authors sought to demonstrate the validity of the reputational approach to the study of community power. Polsby argues that the evidence presented to validate the reputational approach was insufficient to that objective and that the evidence which is presented does not support conclusions the authors reached.

Polsby, Nelson W. "How to Study Community Power: The Pluralist Alternative," *Journal of Politics* 22 (August 1960) 474-84.

It is argued that those who approach the study of power by asking who rules a community beg the bigger question by assuming that someone does rule. The pluralist approach rejects the notion that some group necessarily dominates the community. Polsby explains the various assumptions of the pluralist approach and briefly develops the underpinnings of such assumptions. He then presents a brief outline of the research design which would be necessary to undertake a study of community power.

The author criticizes a number of assumptions which he feels have been made by those who study community power. Specifically, he criticizes those who overlook the fact that the exercise of power takes place in the context of specific issues and that one must study these issues in order to determine who really makes decisions in communities. He argues that because of the issue context of power, the power of any individual or group is likely to be variable over time and to fluctuate with the kinds of decisions which individuals or groups hope to influence. Polsby does not discount the usefulness of asking informed persons to indicate who has influence, but he argues that it is necessary to match the evidence gathered in this way with data on the manner in which those who are allegedly influential participate in making specific decisions.

Polsby, Nelson W. "Power in Middletown: Fact and Value in Community Research," *Canadian Journal of Economics and Political Science* 26 (November 1960) 592-603.

Polsby criticizes the Lynds' studies of "Middletown" (Muncie, Indiana) and states that their analysis was based on a presupposed class struggle. He argues that the Lynds' conclusion that Middletown was dominated by the "X Family" is not supported by the evidence presented, and, in some instances, is actually refuted. He claims that efforts to explain the setbacks to elites, those based on the argument that elites obtain those goals most important to them, cannot be empirically disproven and are therefore of questionable utility.

Polsby, Nelson W., "Three Problems in the Analysis of Community Power," *American Sociological Review* 24 (December 1959) 796-803.

The reputational approach to the study of community power is criticized on the grounds that it is nonempirical. The author suggests that there are three important problems not dealt with by the reputational approach. The first of these problems is to identify those with power. This problem can be dealt with through the study of key decisions within certain issue areas. The second problem is to specify the degree to which the same leaders are influential in different issue areas. Leaders need to be identified in terms of the numbers and types of decisions in which they are involved and whether or not the policy decisions which are finally reached are favorable to the positions which they have taken. The third problem is to determine empirically the degree of cohesion among economic, social status, and political power elites.

Preston, James D. "A Comparative Methodology for Identifying Community Leaders," *Rural Sociology* 34 (December 1969) 556-62.

This study tests three hypotheses drawn from the methodological literature on identifying community leaders: (1) there is a relationship between methods of identifying leaders and results, i.e., reputational studies find elites whereas issue studies find pluralistic leadership structures; (2) differentiated communities appear to have differentiated leadership structures; and (3) each of the different approaches for identifying leaders appears to tap a different dimension of leadership. The investigation, which took place in communities A and B described in the author's "Identification of Community Leaders," involved developing three measures. First, the action or behavioral measure was based on participation in those community action programs over the past five years mentioned by officers of formal organizations, 137 and 230 members of civic clubs in A and B respectively, and officials and employees of the Chamber of Commerce in A and its equivalent in B. Key participants in each program were interviewed as were other people mentioned by those initially interviewed. Second, the reputational measure was derived from nominations by those involved in the community action programs. Third, the "participational" measure was based on the number of offices held by reputational and action leaders in local organizations. The most striking finding was that essentially the same leadership grouping was identified by the different measures used, and thus contradicts the first hypothesis. The second hypothesis was likewise unsubstantiated, because, although the communities differed in a number of ways, they were found to have similar leadership structures. The third hypothesis was partially verified; the action and reputational measures were highly related and measure a similar dimension of leadership, whereas the participational technique appears to measure a different dimension.

Preston, James D. "Identification of Community Leaders," *Sociology and Social Research* 53 (January 1969) 204-16.

This article compares the three major approaches for the identification of community leaders — reputational, decisional, and positional. All three approaches were employed in two southern communities — "A" and "B" — within a single state, which were very similar in terms of population (about 20,000), distance from a metropolitan area (about ninety miles) and proportion of the labor force in agriculture, but differed greatly in terms of racial and ethnic compositions, rate of population increase, and percentage of low-income families and differed slightly in terms of median income and education. The reputational measure was obtained from a panel of informants assumed to be knowledgeable about community affairs (111 in A, and 122 in B); the action measure consisted of a historical reconstruction of the major action programs in each community over the previous five years (twenty-five programs in A, and twenty-four in B); the positional measure consisted of the number of offices held by the respondents in local organizations. The central finding was "the substantial degree of overlap existing among the three approaches for identifying leaders." This finding is supported, the author observes, by similar research projects in small communities, but contradicts the results of investigations in larger communities with more specialized, limited-interest leaders and less visible leadership structures. The substantial overlap in this study, however, suggests that in smaller and middle-sized cities, the results of the three approaches will be the same, particularly with regard to identifying the top grouping of leaders.

Preston, James D. "The Search for Community Leaders: A Re-examination of the Reputational Technique," *Sociological Inquiry* 39 (Winter 1969) 39-47.

The article focuses on the application of a method for identifying leaders similar to Bonjean's modification of the traditional reputational approach (see Charles M. Bonjean, "Community Leadership: A Case Study and Conceptual Refinement," *American Journal of Sociology* 68 [May 1963] 672-81). Preston, within two southern towns — Communities "A" and "B" described in the author's "Identification of Community Leaders," *Sociology and Social Research* 53 (January 1969) 204-16 — obtained reputational nominations from three sources: a panel of community informants, a stratified random sample of residents, and the leaders identified by other respondents. The purpose of the investigation was to test the validity of Bonjean's thesis "that different groups within the community would perceive different individuals as being leaders . . .", and, specifically, his typology which grouped leaders as "concealed," "symbolic," or "visible." The findings indicated, however, that "all three groupings of respondents in these two communities were in very close agreement about the identity of leaders." Further, in contrast with the findings of pluralist political scientists, "the leaders were general rather than specific by issue area." The probable explanation for these differences, the author feels, "is that visibility itself is a variable which varies from community to community." Several community characteristics which may explain leader visibility are discussed.

Rainwater, Lee, and Pittman, David J. "Ethical Problems in Studying a Politically Sensitive and Deviant Community," *Social Problems* 14 (Spring 1967) 357-65.

The authors discuss the ethical problems social scientists must deal with when studying deviant and problem behavior. They relate their observations to research they have undertaken in a large public housing project. Some of the problems dealt with are: confidentiality, relations with the press, relations with subjects in the larger community, and sponsorship.

Reid, Ira DeA., and Ehle, Emily L. "Leadership Selection in Urban Locality Areas," *Public Opinion Quarterly* 14 (Summer 1950) 262-84.

Interviews of a random sample of the residents in twenty-four four-block areas in metropolitan Philadelphia were conducted to determine the way in which different types of people identified community leadership. The sample was chosen to match the characteristics of the total population. The residents of upper-income areas tended to nominate professionals and businessmen while those from lower-income areas tended to nominate politicians. Among all groups, lawyers were attributed substantial status as persons to whom one could turn for reliable advice. Most of the leaders identified by each respondent tended to live in the near vicinity of the respondent.

Rose, Arnold M. "Power Distribution in the Community through Voluntary Association," in J.E. Julett, Jr., and Ross Stayner, eds., *Problems in Social Psychology* (Urbana, Illinois: University of Illinois, 1952) pp. 74-83.

Rossi, Peter H. "Community Decision Making," *Administrative Science Quarterly* 1 (March 1957) 415-43.

The author undertakes a comprehensive analysis of the literature on a study of decision making in American communities and he focuses on the differences in three major approaches used thus far. Those approaches are: (1) the identification of decision makers in terms of their formal institutional position; (2) identification of leadership through participation in decision making; and (3) the definition of leadership in terms of reputation for influence. He suggests that community researchers seek to identify leaders in terms of the types of roles they play, the differences in the institutional and ecological setting of the communities in which those roles are played, and the kinds of issues and processes on which they seek to exert their influence.

Schattschneider, E.E., and Jones, Victor. *Local Political Surveys* (New York: Holt, Rinehart and Winston, 1955).

While this volume does not deal with community power per se, it describes in great detail how one might go about understanding certain aspects of local politics and how one might find and interpret various types of documentary-type evidence concerning the community. Among the subjects dealt with are: the organization and functions of local government; election statistics; the political significance of demographic, social, and economic data; understanding areas and boundaries; the use of census data in the study of congressional and legislative districts in metropolitan areas; population and the local community; and the political economy of the local community.

Schulze, Robert O., and Blumberg, Leonard U. "The Determination of Local Power Elites," *American Journal of Sociology* 63 (November 1957) 290-96.

In this study of "Cibola," Michigan (Ypsilanti, population 20,000) several lists of community leaders were developed, utilizing different methods. First, the reputation for leadership was determined by a panel of voluntary association leaders. Second, leaders were identified by the positions they held in political and civic organizations. Third, a list of economic dominants was formulated, based on the size and wealth of the enterprise owned or managed by individuals.

Few economic dominants were found on the list formulated by the panel of voluntary association leaders. When public leaders and economic dominants were asked to rank leaders, both formulated similar lists and these lists were in turn very similar to those formulated by the voluntary association leaders. No group considered the economic dominants to form a substantial element of the persons of influence in the community. Public leaders were middle class, had lived in the community for a substantial length of time, were actively involved in civic affairs other than those which might be thought of as strictly political, and moreover, as a group, political leaders had relatively frequent social contact with one another.

Seasholes, Bradbury. "Patterns of Influence in Metropolitan Boston: A Proposal for Field Research," in Bert E. Swanson, ed., *Current Trends in Comparative Community Studies* (Kansas City: Community Studies, Inc., 1962) pp. 60-68.

The author formulated a plan for identifying the distribution of influence in sixty-five communities in the Boston metropolitan area and for relating these differing distributions to the structural characteristics in the communities. Patterns of influence are to be determined by the reputational approach, using governmental leaders as those who nominate others in each community as influential. The author is especially concerned with understanding "how metropolitan dynamics may distort patterns of influence that might prevail if component towns and cities were in fact independent." A series of hypotheses concerning the relationship between certain aspects of the distribution of influence in the community and certain structural characteristics of the community are advanced without elaboration.

Smith, Joel, and Hood, Thomas. "The Delineation of Community Power Structures by Reputational Approach," *Sociological Inquiry* 36 (Winter 1966) 3-14.

The authors asked a probability sample of the white population of all but the three lowest socioeconomic status census tracts in a southern city to identify the seven most important people in the community. Those identified were considered a "potential power group" and reputation was viewed as an important power resource.

Those interviewed were divided into five groups by social class. The top group (upper class) was able to make an average of 4.3 choices for leadership positions while the lowest class was able to nominate on the average only 1.29 persons. The three middle groupings by class were about equally effective in nominating leaders. There was high consensus across all groups concerning those who were most often ranked as most influential. Respondents were graded for their ability to select those leaders who had been selected by the consensus and it was found that the most "efficient" respondents were similar in background to the "panels of experts used in other studies using the reputational approach."

Sollie, C.R. "A Comparison of Reputational Techniques for Identifying Community Leaders," *Rural Sociology* 31 (September 1966) 301-09.

Stone, Gregory P., and Form, William H. "Instabilities in Status: The Problem of Hierarchy in the Community Study of Status Arrangements," *American Sociological Review* 18 (April 1953) 149-62.

Sykes, Gresham M. "Differential Distribution of Community Knowledge," *Social Forces* 29 (May 1951) 376-82.

Thernstrom, Stephan. " 'Yankee City' Revisited: The Perils of Historical Naivete," *American Sociological Review* 30 (April 1966) 234-42.

This critical re-examination of Lloyd Warner's "Yankee City" series seeks to detail the distortions which can result from historical ignorance and naivete in sociological research. Although the author notes that the methodological deficiencies in Warner's approach have been criticized, no one has pointed out the extent to which misinterpretations were caused by a failure to utilize relevant historical data. The basic shortcoming in the "Yankee City" study was to reconstruct the past from the perceptions of those interviewed as part of the study. It was impossible to evaluate accurately the causes and significance of events during the study since they were assessed against the background of the mythic past rather than the actual past. For example, Warner's description of a 1933 strike as a radical departure from community traditions caused by the tensions resulting from decreased upward social mobility produced by mechanization overlooks the historical facts that (1) strikes had occurred frequently in the past and (2) that the earlier idealized craft system provided fewer opportunities for upward mobility than did the factory system. The author concludes by asserting that interpretations of the present require a number of assumptions about the past. The issue is whether historical background will be "explicit," based on careful examination of sources or "implicit," rooted in "uncritical acceptance of local mythology."

Vidich, Arthur J.; Bensman, Joseph; and Stein, Maurice R. *Reflections on Community Studies* (New York: John Wiley and Sons, 1964).

  Reviews:

  Polsby, Nelson W., *American Journal of Sociology* 70 (January 1965) 484.

  Mayo, Selz C., *Social Forces* 43 (May 1965) 602-03.

This collection of essays deals with methodological problems in the study of communities. Most of the contributors report on research they conducted on some of the major studies of the community both in the United States and abroad. Among the communities which were the sites of research discussed in this volume are: "Cornerville," "Crestwood Heights," "Plainville," "Springdale," and "Loma." In addition to the editors, the contributors are William F. White, Everett C. Hughes, Morris Schwartz, Stanley Desmond, John R. Seeley, Kurt H. Wolfe, Howard S. Becker, Art Gallagher, Jr. and E. Franklin Frazier. The special concern of this volume is with the difficulties and opportunities which inhere in what loosely may be called the anthropological approach to community studies. The author suggests ways of overcoming the difficulties and making the most of the opportunities presented by this research technique.

Walton, John. "Discipline, Method, and Community Power: A Note on the Sociology of Knowledge," *American Sociological Review* 31 (October 1966) 684-89.

According to the author, four types of methods adequately encompass the variety of procedures which are found in the literature on the study of community power. These techniques are described as: (1) reputational; (2) decision making; (3) the case study; and (4) a combination of the reputational and decision-making approaches. He notes that the positional approach is invariably a part of either the reputational or the decision-making methods. He compares the results of a substantial number of community studies with the methodology used and the academic discipline of the researchers. He finds that political scientists, much more often than sociologists, found more diffused power structures and that the reputational method correlated very highly with findings of highly structured systems of community influence. After controlling for the method used and the discipline of the researcher, Walton concludes that discipline determines the type of research design chosen. He observes that researchers would be well advised to use a combination of research methods and he stresses the need for comparative research.

White, James E. "Theory and Method for Research in Community Leadership," *American Sociological Review* 15 (February 1950) 50-60.

In this study of a rural New York community 105 leaders of community organizations and 176 other persons were interviewed. Each interviewer was asked to indicate individuals he considered to be: (1) most influential, (2) the initiators of action, (3) the most prestigious, (4) the best liked and (5) the most representative. Among other things the author finds that organizational leaders tended to nominate (in all the classifications) persons who held formal positions of leadership more often than did the other citizens.

Wilson, E.K. "Determinants of Participation in Policy Formation in a College Community," *Human Relations* 7 (1954) 287-312.

Wolfinger, Raymond E. "A Plea for Decent Burial," *American Sociological Review* 27 (December 1962) 841-47.

The author reviews the shortcomings of the reputational approach to the study of community power and urges that that approach be interred.

Wolfinger, Raymond E. "Reputation and Reality in the Study of Community Power," *American Sociological Review* 25 (October 1960) 636-44.

Wolfinger thoroughly reviews the literature dealing with the study of community power and argues that the reputational technique of identifying leaders (i.e., the identification of leaders by a panel of "knowledgeables"), assumes that the appearance of power and actual power are equivalent. He examines the various assumptions of the reputational approach and the consequences of the technique itself. He stresses that researchers and respondents use such ambiguous terms as "power" without defining them and there is no way, therefore, to validate the latter's perception of who has influence. He concludes that the findings of a relatively cohesive power elite that characterize most "reputational studies" are an artifact of the technique itself rather than a description of the real world.

DISSERTATIONS

Blome, Arvin Chris. "A Study in the Identification of Community Power Structure and Influence on Public School Issues," Ph.D., State University of Iowa, 1963. (Order No. 63-7989) m $3.00; x $8.60.

Erickson, Eugene C. "The Reputational Technique in a Cross-Community Perspective: Selected Problems of Theory and Measurement," Ph.D., Michigan State University, 1961.

Fox, Roger A. "The Validity and Efficacy of Individual Power Measures for the Study of Community Social Change," Ph.D., University of Illinois at Urbana-Champaign, 1971. (Order No. 71-14, 747) 140 pp.

Jenkins, Quentin A. "Community Actors' Perceptions of Community Power Structure," Ph.D., Iowa State University of Science and Technology, 1966. (Order No. 66-6987) m $3.25; X $11.50.

Preston, James Dene. "A Typology of Community Leadership," Ph.D., Mississippi State University, 1967. (Order No. 67-9208) m $3.00; x $9.00.

Shepard, Morris A. "Community Power Structures: A Typology of Societal Correlates," Ph.D., University of Connecticut, 1969. (Order No. 70-1313) m $3.00; x $7.80. 168 pp.

Shibles, Mark Richard. "Community Power Structures and District School Organization Relationships: An Exploratory Analysis of Input Functions," Ph.D., Cornell University, 1968. (Order No. 68-9448) m $3.20; x $11.25.

Walton, John Thomas. "An Analysis of Methods and Findings in Studies of Community Power Structure," Ph.D., University of California, Santa Barbara, 1966. (Order No. 67-11, 011) m $3.00; x $9.90.

Wilkinson, Kenneth Paul. "A Behavioral Measure of Community Leadership," Ph.D., Mississippi State University, 1965. (Order No. 65-13415) m $3.00; x $7.40.

Chapter 4

EFFORTS AT SYNTHESIS, GENERAL CRITICISM AND OTHER COMMENTARIES

Adrian, Charles R. "Power and City Officials," *Community Leadership and Decision Making* (Iowa City, Iowa: Institute of Public Affairs, University of Iowa, 1966) 35-47.

The author notes that very little is known with any certainty about the economic, social or political factors that are associated with the distribution of political influence in communities. He offers a number of generalizations based on the available literature: (1) economic elites in absentee-owned industry are less likely to be involved in local politics than are the owners and managers of home-owned businesses; (2) power is often functionally defined with relatively narrow boundaries; (3) power structures may generally have been more monolithic a decade or more ago than they are now; (4) government officials play an increasingly dominant role in community decision making; (5) one's place in the power structure of most towns reflects the overall strength of the group for which he is a spokesman; (6) elites do not necessarily form a cohesive group; (7) many vital decisions are not made by government; (8) power is an exhaustible commodity; (9) direct political activity is not, in itself, an effective measure of political power; (10) community power cannot be considered independently of power at the state and national levels.

Adrian, Charles R., ed. *Social Science and Community Action* (East Lansing: Institute for Community Development, Michigan State University, 1960).

This short volume is the proceedings of a conference on community power held at Michigan State University. It includes a short article by Adrian and papers by Robert Dahl and Peter Rossi. (The individual articles are annotated in this bibliography under each author's name.)

Adrian, Charles R. "The Community Setting," in Charles R. Adrian, ed., *Social Science and Community Action* (East Lansing: Institute for Community Development, Michigan State University, 1960) pp. 1-8.

The author notes several characteristics of American communities that "serve as a reference for local decision making." Among the observations made are the following: (1) the term "community" as a symbol of direct social relationships and grass roots government has a loose fit with reality; (2) community projects are of limited value in citizen education; (3) community politics is, in part, an elaborate system of status striving; (4) community decisions are often crisis oriented; (5) specialized professionals play an increasingly dominant role in decision making; (6) the actions of government and of private groups outside the community place limits on local decisions; and (7) value systems play a critical role in decision making even though very little is known about this.

Agger, Robert E.; Swanson, Bert E.; Goldrich, Daniel; and Goldstein, Marshall. "Political Influence Structures: Some Theoretical and Empirical Considerations," in Bert Swanson, ed., *Current Trends in Comparative Community Studies* (Kansas City, Missouri: Community Studies, Inc., 1962) pp. 81-88.

On the basis of their study of four cities of varying size, the authors suggest that political influence may be seen as the function of the relationship between political status and political participation. They emphasize the need for refining measurements of influence. In conclusion, they emphasize the importance of comparative study of community and state. "The major value of this pursuit, as with the measurement and comparison of social class structures, is not − at least initially − for the study of individual behavior, but rather for the study of the political behavior of categories and groups. As social theory of classes, groups and aggregates develops in a comparative frame, theory of individual behavior may be expected to improve . . . . It is in the creation of a hitherto non-existent group or aggregate political theory that comparative community research on political influence promises to pay off."

Agger, Robert E., and Ostrom, Vincent. "Political Participation in a Small Community," in Heinz Eulau, Samuel J. Eldersveld, and Morris Janowitz, eds., *Political Behavior: A Reader in Theory and Research* (Glencoe, Illinois: The Free Press, 1956) pp. 138-48.

The data on which this study is based was gathered from 260 citizens selected at random in a city with a population of 2,000 in the western United States. Respondents were asked to name those most influential in three areas: school affairs, local government and community welfare. Those who participated most actively in community affairs were most able to identify persons as leaders in these areas and generally had more favorable attitudes toward the persons holding leadership positions. Higher rates of political participation were positively correlated with high income and high occupational status and most directly with high educational achievement. The political structure is seen as a communication system with the people of the community playing various roles in the system depending on the amount and quality of their participation. Political roles played by the community citizens are identified in six categories: active advisors, passive advisors, talkers, workers, listeners, and nonparticipants.

Aiken, Michael. "Community Power and Community Mobilization," *Annals of the American Academy of Political and Social Science* 385 (September 1969) 76-88.

This article seeks to answer the question: is the level of citizen participation in public policy making (such participation is called "community mobilization") related to whether power is widely diffused or narrowly concentrated? The author classifies thirty-one previous studies in accordance with a "diffusion-of-power" scale and correlates these conclusions with the amount of citizen participation in four federally supported programs (public housing, urban renewal, "model cities," and the "war on poverty"). He finds greater citizen involvement in community decision making when power is most diffused.

Alford, Robert R. "The Comparative Study of Urban Politics," in Leo Schnore and Henry Fagin, eds., *Urban Research and Policy Planning: Urban Affairs Annual Reviews, Vol. 1* (Beverly Hills, California: Sage Publications, 1967) pp. 263-302.

The author identifies four classes of analytical factors which he suggests will facilitate the comparative analysis of urban political systems. The factors identified are: (1) situational; (2) structural (long-term situations and relatively unchanging elements in society and polity – such as the economic base and the social and economic composition of the community); (3) cultural (qualitative value commitments); and (4) environmental (factors impinging on the community from outside and boundaries of the local political system).

Alford then reviews a number of major books on urban politics and critically examines each book in the context of his paradigm. The books analyzed are: *Men at the Top* by Robert Presthus, *1400 Governments* by Robert Wood, *Four Cities* by Oliver Williams and Charles Adrian; *Suburban Differences and Metropolitan Policies* by Oliver Williams, Thomas Dye, Charles Liebman and Harold Herman; and *The Rulers and the Ruled* by Robert Agger, Daniel Goldrich and Bert Swanson.

Anton, Thomas. "Power Pluralism and Local Politics," *Administrative Science Quarterly* 7 (March 1963) 425-57.

After reviewing various analyses of the reputational approach to the study of community power, the author turns to a lengthy discussion of the weaknesses of the "pluralist approach." He criticizes the pluralist approach on four grounds: (1) one cannot generalize about the general distribution of influence in the community through the study of a limited number of issues; (2) pluralists do not adequately define their concept of "community;" (3) power tends to be defined by pluralists in terms of influence exercised in and by public agencies; (4) the pluralist approach is conflict oriented; in the absence of overt issues pluralists must assume that no power exists; (5) by defining power in terms of personal interaction and ignoring the context of that interaction, the pluralists develop findings which reflect the unsystematic uses of individual power but not "community power."

Anton observes that the differences in the findings of sociologists and political scientists are the result, at least in part, of different views of the community. The sociologist tends to view the community as a system of action. Therefore, he examines the structure of political roles involved in setting community policies. On the other hand, the political scientist sees the community as collections of individuals and attempts to measure, in quantitative terms, the amounts of power held by each individual.

Anton, Thomas. "Rejoinder to Robert Dahl's Critique of 'Power Pluralism and Local Politics,' " *Administrative Science Quarterly* 8 (September 1963) 257-68.

In response to Dahl's criticism that he ignored the findings of Dahl's study of New Haven in his critique of pluralism, Anton undertakes an extensive analysis of *Who Governs?*

Babchuck, Nicholas; Marsey, Ruth; and Gordon, C. Wayne. "Men and Women in Community Agencies, A Note on Power and Prestige," *American Sociological Review* 25 (June 1960) 399-403.

The membership of several boards of social agencies in a large northeastern city is studied. The authors conclude that while women play a relatively small role in the economic and political structure of the community, their participation in the governance of these administrative agencies provides them with access to the decision-making process and hence, power.

Bell, Wendell; Hill, Richard J.; and Wright, Charles R. *Public Leadership* (San Francisco: Chandler Publishing Company, 1961).

In this comprehensive review of the literature on public leadership, the authors seek to relate the lessons to be learned from this material to decision making in education. Included in the volume is an extensive bibliography of the major community power studies up to 1960.

Bonjean, Charles M., and Olson, David M. "Community Leadership: Directions of Research," *Administrative Science Quarterly* 9 (December 1964) 278-300.

The authors critically discuss the various approaches to the study of community power and conclude that a combination of techniques seems to offer the greatest research payoffs. Rather than classifying community power structures in traditional terms of elitist or pluralist, the author suggests that leadership structures may be classified along four dimensions: legitimacy, vis ility, scope of the decision-maker's influence, and cohesiveness.

The authors observe that descriptions of community power structures should be related to a number of different factors including: (1) the institutional structure of the community; (2) demographic and socioeconomic characteristics of the community; and (3) the consequences of decisions in terms of such measures as effectiveness, efficiency, and the quality of community projects, organizations or institutions.

Burtenshaw, Claude J. "The Political Theory of Pluralist Democracy," *Western Political Quarterly* 21 (December 1968) 577-87.

While this article is essentially a critique of pluralist theory in general, the substance of the article focuses on studies of community power, especially that of Robert Dahl. The thrust of the argument is that pluralists overstate the extent to which access to political decision making is available throughout the population. In support of this critique the author cites the fact that riots and rebellions have struck a substantial number of American cities, including New Haven, Connecticut, "the home of pluralism."

Cahill, Robert S., and Hencley, Stephen, eds. *The Politics of Education* (Danville, Ill.: The Interstate Printers and Publishers, Inc.) 1964.
Five of the articles included in this volume deal directly with community power.
Stephen P. Hencley, "The Study of Community Politics and Power," pp. 5-26.
Luvern L. Cunningham, "Community Power; Implication for Education." pp. 27-50.
William D. Knill, "Community Decision Processes: Research Strategies," pp. 77-92.
Ralph B. Kimbrough, "Development of a Concept of Social Power," pp. 93-110.
David W. Minar, "Community Characteristics, Conflict and Power Structures," pp. 125-44.

Clark, Terry N., ed. *Community Structure and Decision-Making: Comparative Analyses* (San Francisco: Chandler Publishing Co., 1968).
  Reviews:
    Kadushin, Charles, *Political Science Quarterly* 85 (December 1970) 699-702.
    Powers, Ronald C., *Rural Sociology* 34 (September 1969) 418.
    Miller, Delbert C., *American Journal of Sociology* 74 (May 1969) 742.
    Friesma, H. Paul, *Public Administration Review* 30 (September - October 1970) 571-77.
    Johnston, R.C., *Journal of Politics* 29 (February 1967) 1118.
This book is comprised of twenty-two essays, six of which have been contributed by the editor. Most of the essays have appeared elsewhere though some of these were revised for this volume.
The first part of the book is written by Clark and deals with a number of conceptual and definitional problems in community power research. Utilizing the existing literature, including essays by Clark, Rossi and Gilbert, he attempts to develop a series of propositions dealing with the relationship between patterns of decision making and structural characteristics of communities.
The middle sections of the book deal, for the most part, with case studies examining specific kinds of issues and how the values and structures of the communities studied influenced the issue outcomes.
The final sections include discussions of "intercommunity relations and decision making" and an essay by Clark on future research directions.

Clark, Terry N. "Power and Community Structure: Who Governs Where and When?" *The Sociological Quarterly* 8 (Summer 1967) 291-316.
Drawing on the literature dealing with community power and on related sociological theory, Clark formulates thirty-two propositions which seek to explain why the distribution of influence varies from community to community. Clark fits these propositions to a structural-functional typology, utilizing the "AGIL" variables generally associated with Bales and Parsons.

Crain, Robert L., and Rosenthal, Donald B. "Community Status as a Dimension of Local Decision Making," *American Sociological Review* 32 (December 1967) 970-84.

The authors examine the outcomes of eight different types of community issues (urban renewal, school desegregation, bond referenda, fluoridation controversies, political party structures, Negro registration in the South, election contests and civil rights movements). The number of cities studied varied with the type of issue from 8 to 763. They conclude that middle-class cities (as measured by educational attainment) are partly immobilized by high levels of citizen participation in public decision making, which prevent government from exercising authority to make decisions. They also found evidence in a number of cases that this generalization does not hold for cities at the high end of the educational distribution. They conclude that in these cities the educational level is high enough to permit a decision-making process in which citizens play structured, consistent and predictable roles.

Dahl, Robert A. "Reply to Thomas Anton's 'Power Pluralism and Local Politics,' " *Administrative Science Quarterly* 8 (September 1963) 250-56.

In response to an article by Thomas Anton criticizing the "pluralist approach" to the study of community power *(Administrative Science Quarterly* 7 [March 1963] 425-57), Dahl argues that Anton has misinterpreted and misrepresented a number of points.

Dahl, Robert A. "The Analysis of Influence in Local Communities," in Charles R. Adrian, ed., *Social Science and Community Action* (East Lansing: Institute for Community Development, Michigan State University, 1960) pp. 25-42.

In this paper, presented to a seminar on community power at Michigan State University, Dahl sets forth some theoretical assumptions which guide the search for answers to the questions: Who mainly influences political decisions? How? and Why? Dahl suggests that these answers depend on examining four variables: the distribution of influence, the patterns of influence, the extent of conflict and cohesiveness among the influentials, and the sources of, and resistance to, changes in the political system. He outlines a number of hypotheses which follow from his analysis.

D'Antonio, William V. "Community Leadership and Economic Crisis: Testing Ground for Ideological Cleavage," *American Journal of Sociology* 71 (May 1966) 688-700.

Political and economic leaders in South Bend, Indiana were identified by positions they hold in formal organizations and by a panel of "knowledgeables." The author finds that Republicans are more hostile than Democrats to economic assistance by the federal government in a period of economic crisis in the community. But among Republicans, business leaders were more responsive to the idea of federal assistance than were political leaders.

D'Antonio, William V., and Ehrlich, Howard J., eds. *Power and Democracy in America* (Notre Dame, Indiana: University of Notre Dame Press, 1961).

Reviews:
Rose, Arnold M., *Sociology Quarterly* 3 (April 1962) 147-48.
Berger, Monroe, *American Sociological Review* 28 (Spring 1963) 273.
James, Bernard J., "The Issue of 'Power'," *Public Administration Review* 24 (March 1964) 47-51. .
Wrong, Dennis H., *American Sociological Review* 28 (February 1963) 144-45.
Snyder, Eloise C., *Social Forces* 41 (March 1963) 321.

This volume reports on a symposium in which the key participants were Peter Drucker, Delbert C. Miller and Robert Dahl. The essays by Miller and Dahl deal directly with community power. Miller argues that power in cities and towns is largely in the hands of economic elites who operate outside the institutions of government and are not responsive or accountable politically. Dahl argues that American cities are typically pluralistic and he places his analysis in historical perspective.

The editors contribute two chapters in which they summarize the proceedings and raise or clarify issues. In addition, a transcript of a discussion between the participants is included and this provides for a direct confrontation of competing views of society and of how communities should be studied.

Dusek, Val. "Falsifiability and Power Elite Theory," *Journal of Comparative Administration* 1 (August 1969) 198-212.

The author considers the arguments of Dahl ("A Critique of the Ruling Elite Model") and Merelman ("On the Neo-Elitist Critique of Community Power") that the power elite and "false consensus" theories of Mills, Bachrach, and Baratz are non-scientific because they are non-falsifiable. He feels that the charge of non-falsifiability is inconsistent with the methodology of most political scientists, which stresses the heuristic nature of models and theories. To be consistent, therefore, political scientists must apply standards uniformly. This will mean accepting Mills' theory as scientific or else will require the rejection of much contemporary behavioral political science as non-falsifiable, along with Mills' theory.

Fisher, Sethard. "Community Power Studies: A Critique," *Social Research* 29 (Winter 1962) 449-66.

The author reviews a number of studies of community power and suggests that power structure varies with the following: (1) the degree of stability in community life; (2) the value orientations of community leaders; (3) the nature of the community's economic institutions; and (4) the degree of the community's dependence on outside sources for vital goods and services.

Form, William H., and Sauer, Warren L. "Organized Labor's Image of Community Power Structure," *Social Forces* 38 (May 1960) 332-41.

Labor leaders in Lansing, Michigan (population 100,000) who were selected on the nomination of a panel of "knowledgeables" were interviewed by the authors. The consensus among these leaders was that community affairs were dominated by the business sector in the community but that labor leaders did play a role in the power structure. They tended to see themselves not as a group which took leadership in policy making but as a group with which the business-dominated power structure would have to deal if the proposals were to be implemented. There was a general recognition that labor could and should increase its influence in community affairs. On the whole, the labor leaders were relatively sanguine about the types of proposals and general community leadership that came from the business community.

Forward, Roy. "Issue Analysis in Community Power Studies," *Australian Journal of Political History* 15 (December 1969) 26-44.

In order to analyze the community power structure by studying community issues, it is necessary to establish criteria for the "communityness" of issues and for the importance of issues. The author reviews the extensive literature on the study of community power to show how such criteria can be established. The author also discusses ways to insure that the issues selected are a representative sample of community issues, and not just those which are formally resolved. Community leadership, the author concludes, is "more than the ability to prevail on important community issues after they have arisen."

Gilbert, Claire W. "Some Trends in Community Politics: A Secondary Analysis of Power Structure Data from 166 Communities," *Southwestern Social Science Quarterly* 48 (December 1967) 373-81.

Based on the data and methods described in the annotation immediately below, various trends in community politics are examined. The author reaches the following conclusion: "The evidence supports the notion that increasing scalants of society are reflected in the power structure of local communities. It appears that power, i.e., the ability to make binding decisions for the community is less and less in the hands of a privileged few and increasingly dependent upon the broker, be he elected official or not, who can bring together (to the extent he can bring together) the various elements in the community."

Gilbert, Claire. "The Study of Community Power: A Summary and Test" in Scott Greer and David Minar, eds., *The New Urbanization* (New York, St. Martin's Press, 1968) pp. 222-45.

After a brief review of the literature on community power and a summary of some of the problems involved, the author focuses her attention on the question of whether differences in the community studied or in the methodology and conceptualization used are the primary determinants in the differences in the distribution of power in American communities that have been found by researchers. She bases her analysis on 166 studies of influence in decision making in American cities. After introducing a number of "quality controls" to the data she extracts from these studies, and controlling for the size of the community studied and the discipline of the investigator (political scientists/sociologists) she concludes that: (1) the distribution of power between "informals" and politicians is closely related to size, the larger cities being much more likely to be dominated by politicians; and (2) that the discipline of the researcher is a reasonably good predictor of the findings of these studies, with political scientists more likely to find communities dominated by politicians.

Gitlin, Todd. "Local Pluralism as Theory and Ideology," *Studies on the Left* 5 (1965) 21-45.

It is argued that local pluralism is a coherent theory with its own methodology and critique of the rival "stratification" model. As a theory, local pluralism is inadequate and faulty for several reasons: (1) because it tries too hard to avoid the attributed difficulties of the stratification models, (2) because of methodological difficulties, (3) because its definition and assumptions dictate its conclusions, and (4) because it is willfully blind to the proper purposes of the study of power. Gitlin charges that local pluralism tends to justify the status quo and he urges an alternative theory of community power be developed which facilitates the identification of those scopes of power with respect to which the power balance must and can be shifted and how such shifts might be achieved.

Goldstein, Marshall N. "Absentee Ownership and Monolithic Power Structures: Two Questions for Community Studies," in Bert E. Swanson, ed., *Current Trends in Comparative Community Studies* (Kansas City: Community Studies Inc., 1962) pp. 49-59.

The author suggests that findings indicating the involvement in the local community of business executives who are the agents of nonresident owners create a need to reformulate the hypothesis that economic dominants are likely to play a minor role in communities whose economic structure is dominated by absentee-owned industry. He suggests that when absentee-owned industries are of an extractive nature, and require either raw materials or labor resources which are unique to the area, they will have sufficient stake in the community to become involved in its politics. Further, it is hypothesized that relatively new firms, whether they are home-owned or not, have few commitments to the local area and thus their executives are less likely to be involved in the community than are the executives of older, locally-owned firms.

Goldstein also argues that while the pluralists have criticized the reputational approach for assuming cohesion among top elites, they are subject to the criticism that they assume differences among leaders which are not always empirically verified. He argues that researchers should examine the degree to which leaders have common interests, the division of interests between group spokesmen and members, and whether or not leaders share the basic values of the people for whom they speak.

Hawley, Willis, and Wirt, Frederick, eds. *The Search for Community Power* (Englewood Cliffs, N.J.: Prentice-Hall, 1968).

Reviews:

Corwin, R. David, *American Journal of Sociology* 76 (July 1970) 182-86.

Scoble, Harry M., *American Sociological Review* 35 (April 1970) 589.

Friesma, H. Paul, *Public Administration Review* 30 (September/October 1970) 571-79.

This collection of readings brings together many of the best-known and most widely discussed articles on community power. There are twenty-nine items organized in terms of: "The Notion of Power," "Community Power: Ruling Elite Models," "Community Power: the Pluralist Perspective," "Locating Decision

Makers: Alternative Strategies," "Some Continuing Problems in the Search for Power," and "Toward a Theory of Community Power — Future Research Directions." Each section and each article is preceded by editors' commentary.

Herson, Lawrence J. "In the Footsteps of Community Power," *American Political Science Review* 55 (December 1961) 817-30.

The author reviews the literature on community power and seeks to relate the findings therein to the interests of political scientists. He reviews the weaknesses of the reputational approach to the study of community power but suggests that its relative ease of administration and its transportability from community to community are arguments for its continued use. In Herson's words, "like Henry Ford, Hunter has found the secret of mass production . . . Hunter's technicians are freed from both the need of residency in their community and the need to create holistic studies." He also suggests that studies by Delbert Miller and Robert Hanson, which have demonstrated that the findings of the reputational approach can be used to predict the outcome of community decisions, tend to support the validity of the method.

Herson argues that political scientists would do well to utilize the findings of community power studies to understand better the political phenomena in which they have been traditionally interested. For example, he suggests that the relationships between the structure of community power and the following variables be investigated: (1) the type of party system in the community; (2) the dimensions of political participation; (3) size and urbanization of the community; and (4) certain political institutions such as the short ballot, the weak-mayor system, and the council-manager form of government.

Hunter, Floyd. *The Big Rich and the Little Rich* (Garden City, New York: Doubleday, 1965).

Reviews:
    Williams, J. Allen, *American Sociological Review* 31 (April 1966) 293-94.

This book is a compilation of essays on the subject of great personal wealth in the United States. Observations are drawn from two communities — "Ivydale," a small southeastern university town, and the Bay area of California.

Hunter, Floyd. "Power is Where You Find It," *Adult Leadership* 3 (May 1954) 4-5 and 31-32.

Janowitz, Morris. "Community Power and 'Policy Science' Research," *Public Opinion Quarterly* 26 (Fall 1962) 398-410.

In this review article, the author critically analyzes the findings and methodology used in two studies, *Political Influence* by Edward C. Banfield and *Who Governs?* by Robert A. Dahl. Janowitz suggests that future community power studies should attempt to overcome two basic deficiencies in the books reviewed. First, there is a need for comparative studies; and, second, research should be relevant to policy decisions. He recommends focusing attention on what happens in communities when social experiments are introduced, such as the adoption of a birth control program. He also suggests that various experimental approaches such as organized group discussions with community leaders might be of some utility.

Kaufman, Herbert, and Jones, Victor. "The Mystery of Power," *Public Admin-istrative Review* 14 (Summer 1954) 205-12.

In this extended review of Hunter's *Community Power Structure,* the authors consider the nature of power and criticize Hunter for adding little to previous literature on the subject of power. Hunter's description of the social structure of "Regional City" may or may not be accurate, they feel, but this is beside the point if the methods used to arrive at this description are faulty. Basically, the authors contend, Hunter has presupposed the very point which must be proved, i.e., that a power elite exists. Hunter fails to show that the activities of the top leaders necessarily determine the course of events in Regional City (i.e., that the same events would not occur without their presence) or that the power relationship is not symmetrical, and in fact, there is evidence in this book that the top leaders must engage in bargaining to a degree inconsistent with their supposed power. Further, Hunter overlooks the importance in decision making of bureaucratic groups which choose issues and alter and make policy, because he equates the public support of a specific plan with the power over that entire decision. Rather than being a study of the power structure, the authors assert that the book is actually "a portrait of one of the groups having some power over some things at some times" in what may be, in fact, a pluralist society.

Keynes, Edward, and Ricci, David M., eds. *Political Power, Community and Democracy* (Chicago: Rand McNally & Co., 1970).

This reader is composed of nine selections published previously and four original essays by the authors, to be discussed below. The material is grouped into three sections: first, actual power studies and selections on the background to those studies by Latham, Truman, Hunter, Mills, and Dahl; second, methodoiogical problems with selections by Polsby and Bachrach and Baratz; and third, selections by Mayo and Davis which evaluate the facts of community power as they relate to democracy.

In "Background to the Study of Community Power: Liberalism, Its Decline, Power Analysis, Schumpeter, and After," Ricci attributes the interest in studying power in community politics to the declining faith in traditional liberalism. As fundamental premises in the liberal view have come under attack by social scientists, scholars have turned their attention to manifestations of power. As a guide to inquiry, the theoretical framework which replaced liberalism was the "process theory" of democracy. This approach represents, in the author's opinion, a "reconstructed liberalism." The article is concluded with a discussion of the attacks upon the validity of basic premises of the process theory.

In "Methodological Disputes in the Study of Power," Ricci reviews and analyzes the three major methods for locating power — reputational, positional and decisional — and the controversy over the proper definitions of key terms in that search. He concludes with a familiar adage: that the questions men ask determine the answers they obtain. Because the method of investigation, in the author's opinion, is associated with the findings, he suggests a corollary to the old adage which summarizes his commentary on the controversy over methods: "The answers men seek determine the questions they ask." The proponents of different approaches — roughly political scientists who prefer the decisional approach, on the one hand, and sociologists, on the other — are men of "conflicting outlook and social persuasion." The differences in outlook "predispose them to be satisfied or dissatisfied with society and, thereby, determine the shape of their inquiries."

In "Democracy and Community Power," Ricci reviews and analyzes the significance of central themes in the literature on community power as they pertain to democracy. The central question is: do the facts of community power equate with democracy? Such facts are subject to differing interpretations depending upon one's categories for normative evaluation. The author sets forth a basic distinction between a view of democracy which emphasizes functional rationality, process and stability, on the one hand, and substantive rationality, ends, and the good life, on the other. He identifies two loose groups of scholars with opposing viewpoints, which he labels the advocates — those who accept and endorse the existing facts of group politics, business influence, elite powers, low rates of participation and high rates of apathy: and the adversaries — those who express dissatisfaction with present conditions. Although the views of the former constitute a sort of "academic orthodoxy," the author basically supports the case made by the adversaries.

In "Elites and Community Power," Keynes reviews the literature on elites in terms of several central questions around which the debate among scholars has revolved — what does the term elite mean, what is the composition of the elite, in what ways does it exercise power, and what is the relation between elite and mass in society? A final question implicit in the others is also considered, i.e., what are the consequences for this debate for the continuing formulation of liberal democratic thought? The author then reviews the work of writers representative of various approaches to the study of elites: Michaels, Mills, Mosca, Ostrogorskii, Pareto, Sorokin, Lasswell, Truman, and Dahl.

Killian, Lewis M. "Community Structure and the Role of the Negro Leader-Agent,"
    Sociological Inquiry 35 (Winter 1965) 69-79.

In this review of literature, the author focuses on differences in the structure of white and Negro sub-communities. This is a variable which, apart from the superior power of the white sub-community, may affect the progress of desegregation. The institutional structure of the Negro community is a "weak and inferior imitation of the wider, essentially white communities," with only labor unions and protest organizations coming close to exerting real power in the Negro community. Because of the differences between the Negro and white community, Negro leader-agents in their contacts with the bureaucratized white community structure suffer several disadvantages in pressing demands with the appropriate specialist in the white sub-system. First, they are non-experts concerned with rapid fulfillment of general demands who must deal with an expert in the area of activity at issue. Second, the Negro leader-agent is frustrated by the "stablizing, yet conservatizing, influence of the complex, bureaucratic community structure," which both limits the freedom of the individual white spokesman and provides the opportunity for evasive action by appealing to the sub-system he represents. Third, because the Negro community has no formal structure, it is difficult for the Negro leader to establish his legitimacy as a spokesman whereas the role of the white agent is defined by his position in the formal structure of the sub-system for which he speaks. Fourth, successful negotiations are hampered by the supposed need for one sub-system to concur in the actions of another. Confronted with such a diffuse decision-making structure, the Negro leader is likely to oversimplify the community structure and approach it at the point of government only. This strategy is probably self-defeating at the local level because it forces government to abandon its role as neutral agency of social control and become instead the defender of the status quo in all sub-systems of the community.

Laquan, Aprodicio A. *The City in Nation Building* (Manila: School of Public Administration, University of Phillipines, 1966).

Long, Norton E. "The Corporation, Its Satellites and the Local Community," in Edward S. Mason, ed. *The Corporation in Modern Society* (Cambridge: Harvard University Press, 1959) pp. 202-17.

While the corporation in many communities is a basic and central component of the social structure, its influence in local politics has declined. Whether absentee-owned or not, businesses are conscious of antagonizing public opinion and no longer enjoy the close relationships they once enjoyed with local merchants or with political leaders. The business executive is likely to give the corporation his primary loyalty. With the exception of "do gooder-type acts," community affairs are of little interest to the corporation executive. In the author's view, the reintegration of the corporation elites into the local social and political structure is a major problem with which most communities must deal.

Long, Norton E. "The Local Community as an Ecology of Games," *American Journal of Sociology* 64 (November 1958) 251-61.

The author conceptualizes local decision making as an ecology of games of varying salience to the community as a whole and with varying degrees of overlap between the participants of different games. Special emphasis is put on the social interdependence of various games and how one might utilize this interdependence to understand community politics. The author also employs notions of role theory in his analysis and he observes that the allocation of values which results from the decision-making process is in an important way a function of the expectations and self-images of the decision-makers. He argues further that many "community decisions are the somewhat accidental result of unplanned, uncoordinated, activity of various individuals and groups, with the final outcome intended by no one." He stresses the importance of "civic staff men as integrators who mobilize or put together the influence of others to secure action on community projects."

Long, Norton E. "Who Makes Decisions in Metropolitan Areas?" *The Polity* (Chicago, Illinois: Rand McNally and Company, 1962) pp. 156-64.

Long argues that when looking at metropolitan regions as a whole we should think in terms of "who makes decisions that have a significant impact on metropolitan problems?" rather than "who makes decisions which solve metro-politan problems?" He describes the metropolitan area as a "kind of natural governmental ecology in which institutions, groups and governments have de-veloped a system of unintended cooperation through which things get done and the area considered as a system functions." From this conceptual framework he goes on to examine the variety of interests concerned with specific kinds of problems which regularly confront metropolitan areas. He concludes that, "the decisions then that may be most important in our metropolitan areas are economic, piecemeal, harmonized if at all by market forces."

Long, Norton E. "Community Decision Making," in *Community Leadership and Decision Making* (Iowa City, Iowa: Institute of Public Affairs, University of Iowa, 1966) pp. 1-10.

Long observes that American communities are characterized less by power structure than by an absence of power to deal with important problems. He notes that the literature on community power often talks about decision making in terms of decisions which are of little consequence to the community, or to the society as a whole. He notes that community decision making becomes increasingly difficult as attention shifts from physical problems to social problems. He goes on to say that urban problems are not likely to be solved without the combination of national resources in a local government of at least metropolitan scope.

Mann, Lawrence D. "Studies in Community Decision Making," *Journal of the American Institute of Planners* 30 (February 1960) 58-65.

This article reviews a number of the best-known studies dealing with community power and seeks to identify some of the major problems involved in such research. The author argues that many of the findings are affected by the intrusion of preconceptions in the research design and in the conclusions reached.

McKee, James B. "Community Power and Strategies in Race Relations," *Social Problems* 6 (Winter 1958-59) 195-203.

Merelman, Richard M. "On the Neo-Elitist Critique of Community Power," *American Political Science Review* 62 (June 1968) 451-60.

The author extends the arguments raised by critics of the pluralist approach to the study of community power by such scholars as Peter Bachrach and Morton Baratz who hold that a focus on the study of specific decisions overlooks the possibility that power is maintained by "non-decision making." Merelman seeks to show that the critics of the pluralist approach do not offer alternative conceptualizations or methodologies which allow one to discover the distribution and patterns of community influence in ways other than those already employed by the pluralists.

Miller, Delbert C. "Power, Complementarity and the Cutting Edge of Research," *Sociological Focus* 1 (Summer 1963) 1-17.

The author, having reviewed community power literature, examines the two contradictory explanations of power that emerge from earlier writings – the "covert-monolithic" theory and the "overt-pluralist" theory. He asserts that the contradiction between the two can be resolved by applying the principle of complementarity (as physicists have done to manage the conflict between the particle and wave theories of light), which recognizes that the two theories may be employed separately to describe different aspects of the world. "The world is subtler than man's understanding, and the contradictions the scientist uncovers in studying nature lie not in nature itself but simply in man's own inadequate concepts." In identifying leadership structures, researchers should; (1) consider four characteristics – legitimacy, visibility, scope of influence, and cohesiveness, (2) treat each characteristic as a continuum rather than a dichotomous variable, and (3) ascertain the variation in each dimension separately rather than assuming that variation in one (e.g., broad scope) will be associated with variation in another (e.g., cohesiveness.) Finally, the author suggests replacing concepts with operational definitions in the following areas: community power and the accompanying structure, solidarity of top leaders, inter-institutional linkages and collective institutional and organizational power.

Miller, Paul A. "The Process of Decision Making within the Context of Community Organization," *Rural Sociology* 17 (June 1952) 153-61.

The author collected data from 218 officials in a number of small communities in the northeast and southeastern sections of the United States and from case studies in selected areas. He concludes that the basis for social influence in securing public health objectives appeared to be different in each of the two regions. He found that in the northeast, sources of influence appeared to be more informal and to be based on social and economic status, as well as personal skills and knowledge. On the other hand, in the southeast decision-makers tended to hold positions of formal authority and seemed to perceive less need to appeal to the public at large for support.

Newton, K. "A Critique of the Pluralist Model," *Acta Sociologica* 12, No. 4, 209-23.

The purpose of this article is to explore the meaning of the concept "pluralism." The author asserts that the scholars who use the concept have not adequately specified the necessary and sufficient conditions of a pluralist society. Much of the pluralist literature is "not so much pluralist as anti-elitist," with the objective being more to prove that elitism does not exist than to prove that pluralism does. The author critically reviews pluralist literature, especially the work of Dahl, and concludes that Dahl's findings about New Haven are not very different from those of the elitists. The central difference is the way findings are interpreted. Dahl is, in the author's opinion, satisfied that conditions in New Haven – even though it is run by a very small number of individuals whose power and control is not effectively challenged – approximate what is expected of a democratic society. Hunter, on the other hand, was critical of politics in Atlanta because it fell short of the democratic ideal. The debate between them, the author feels, is "not so much between social scientists as between ideologists."

Nix, Harold L. "Concepts of Community and Community Leadership," *Sociology and Social Research* 53 (July 1969) 500-510.

The author's purpose is to offer a conceptualization of (1) community and (2) community leadership. The view taken is that "community" is found in the relationships between the various special-interest groups and organizations within a locality. ("The social facts of which communities are made are the relationships . . .") The "interstitial" or "in-between" relationships fall into two basic types, exchange and coordinative. The author's hypothesis is that whereas individuals tend to gain or lose potential community power through exchange relations, the *exercise* of real community influence depends on their involvement in key coordinative interstitial groups. Communities, the author concludes, are based on competitive or conjunctive relationships, and not on cooperation among groups and individuals. The second half of the article classifies types of leaders and forms of leadership on three dimensions: level and functions, scope of influence, and basic orientation. Several forms of community power are grouped into four categories: focused or unitary, split or bifactional, multifactional, and amorphous.

Parenti, Michael. "Power and Pluralism: A View from the Bottom," *Journal of Politics* 32 (August 1970) 501-30.

Central aspects of the pluralist theory are critically examined in this article, especially the notion that in America the opportunities for the exercise of power are inclusively rather than exclusively distributed and that "neither the enjoyment of dominance nor the suffering of deprivation is the constant condition of any one group." The author then literally views the urban power structure from the bottom by presenting descriptive case studies of three disputes between the Newark Community Union Project − a neighborhood social-protest movement − and landlords, party leaders, the police and city officials. He concludes that there is a broad division in Newark and the other cities with large poor populations between the powerless on the bottom, who have been ignored by previous studies of community power, and the potentially powerful whose competing organizations have been the focus of established research and the basis for the observation that influence is pluralistically distributed in American society. What impresses the powerless, writes Parenti, has been the "remarkable capacity of the plurality of actors and interests" to "move in the same direction against some rather modest lower-class claims."

Polsby, Nelson W. "'Pluralism' in the Study of Community Power, or *Erklarung* before *Verklarung* in *Wissenssociologie*," *American Sociologist* 4 (May 1969) 118-22.

The author attempts to clarify the meanings of "pluralism" made obscure, in his opinion, by the imprecise attacks of critics and to defend pluralism from its detractors, especially the *Wissenssociologen* (represented by Terry N. Clark, et al., "Discipline, Method, Community Structure, and Decision Making: The Role and Limitations of the Sociology of Knowledge," *American Sociologist* 3 [August, 1968] 214-217). He distinguishes among the three meanings of the term. Pluralism$_1$ refers to ecletic methods of gathering data, "generally anthropological or journalistic in character" and organized as case studies. Pluralism$_2$ refers to propositions purporting to describe a certain state of affairs in one or more local communities, specifically, the claim that power in communities is dispersed in various ways. Pluralism$_3$ refers to an intellectual tradition in American political theory which is based on assumptions about human nature, such as the belief that "for political purposes men may belong to groups, but in America rarely classes . . ."

The author sees no connection between any of the three dimensions of the term. Pluralist methodology does not necessarily lead to pluralist empirical findings. The belief in pluralist theories of man does not necessitate use of techniques or bias the outcome of research. Having provided a tongue-in-cheek "scorecard" for orientations to the study of community power, the author counter-attacks by accusing the *Wissenssociologen* of "heaping good studies and bad indiscriminantly into a statistical sausage machine" and coming out with an account of the dispersion or concentration of community power which is suspect, and "therefore, 'explanations' of these semi-fictional distributions are premature."

Prince, Julius S. "The Health Officer and Community Power Groups," *Health Education Monographs* No. 2 (1958) 16-31.

Rabinovitz, Francine F. "Sound and Fury Signify Nothing? A Review of Community Power Research in Latin America," *Urban Affairs Quarterly* 3 (March 1968) 111-22.

The author warns that methodology which may be appropriate for the discovery of leadership in North American cities may be inappropriate in the Latin American context. She discusses the impact of differential cultural traditions on the analysis of community power structure and stresses the importance and difficulty of identifying forces which operate to set limits on decisions in communities. She points out, for example, that the Catholic Church, though its individual clergy may not be involved in decision making, is often an important element in the power equation. She suggests general hypotheses derived from various case studies on Latin American community power: (1) community power structures vary with the stage of economic development; (2) there is a movement generally from fusion or oligarchy to bifurcation within the power structure, bifurcation, that is, between the political and nonpolitical leadership; (3) the shape of community power may be oligarchic but it is not a single pyramid or a monolith; and (4) community power structure is in large part dependent on the nature and demands of national political systems (special emphasis is placed on the nature of the party system and the degree to which it extends to the local level). The author concludes by stressing the need to relate findings and the patterns of leadership with policy outputs.

Reiss, Albert J., Jr. "Some Logical and Methodological Problems in Community Research," *Social Forces* 33 (October 1954) 51-57.

The author distinguishes between the comparative and the community context approaches to the study of communities. He discusses the advantages of each and notes that the comparative approach is most helpful for experimental purposes while the context approach facilitates the isolation of specific community phenomena. The author notes that comparative community research and comparison among community studies is made more difficult by: (1) the absence of a theory of community power, (2) the lack of standard understandings of concepts and definitions and, (3) the failure of studies to examine certain basic, common variables among communities. The author is critical of community studies on a number of other grounds as well: (1) they ignore the external environment of the community; (2) they tend to overgeneralize their findings on the one hand and to particularize from general findings on the other; (3) they do not fully account for change; and (4) they tend to lack time perspective.

Rogers, David. "Community Political Systems: A Framework and Hypothesis for Comparative Studies," in Bert E. Swanson, ed., *Current Trends in Comparative Community Studies* (Kansas City: Community Studies, Inc., 1962) pp. 31-48.

The author sets as his objective the formulation of a framework that would facilitate comparative research on community power structures. The author reviews the various approaches used in community research and evaluates the utility of each in the comparative study of communities. He suggests ways in which certain shortcomings of each method might be resolved.

Rogers dichotomizes political systems into monolithic and pluralistic categories. Drawing on a review of the substantive findings of community power studies, as well as from the community literature more generally, the author formulates some hypotheses dealing with conditions under which each type is likely to exist. He suggests that the following elements of the community social structure are positively related to more pluralistic systems: (1) a high degree of industrialization; (2) large population; (3) a high degree of heterogeneity of population along ethnic, religious and occupational lines; (4) a high degree of differentiation of the polity from kinship and economic systems; (5) extensive scope of government; (6) more than one political party active in the community; and (7) the extensive unionization of blue collar workers (and/or political and economic organizations of working class groups). He goes on to suggest briefly some of the implications of these hypotheses in terms of future research.

Rogers, David. "Urban Power Structures," in *Creativity and Innovation in Manpower Research and Action Programs,* Proceedings of the 3rd Annual Summer Research Institute, Industrial Relations Center (Ames, Iowa: Iowa State University, 1970).

Rossi, Peter H. "Power and Community Structure," *Midwest Journal of Political Science* 4 (November 1960) 390-401.

The author notes the significant range of the findings in the studies of community power and deplores the absence of comparative research. He sets for himself the task of establishing a conceptual scheme for the political structure of local communities. The first step in this scheme is to identify four distinct types of community power structure: (1) pyramidal; (2) caucus rule (decision making involves the development of consent among the "cozy few" who make up the caucus); (3) polylithic (separate power structures definable for major spheres of community activity); and (4) amorphous (no discernible enduring pattern of power).

Rossi summarizes a series of expected relationships between the distribution of influence in the community and certain community characteristics in the form of a general hypothesis. His hypothesis holds that "in communities with partisan electoral procedures whose officials are full-time functionaries, where party lines tend to coincide with class and status lines, and where a party favored by lower-class and status groups has some good chance of getting elected to office, community power structures tend to be polylithic, rather than monolithic."

Rossi, Peter H. "Theory, Research, and Practice in Community Organization," in Charles R. Adrian, ed., *Social Science and Community Action* (East Lansing: Institute for Community Development, Michigan State University, 1960) pp. 9-23.

Basing his observations on a review of the literature of community power, as well as research he has undertaken in six American communities, the author offers a number of observations concerning the social structure of American communities. He notes that all communities are characterized by an overall pyramidal structure of *potential* power, but not necessarily of exercised power. Among the resources which provide the bases for potential power are: (1) control over wealth and other resources; (2) control over the mass media; (3) control over solidary groups; (4) control over values (incumbency of social positions such as the clergy and certain professions which are concerned with the interpretation of cultural values); and (5) control over prestigious interaction. He notes that much potential power is only intermittently exercised. "By and large a city council goes its own way; the mayor himself makes a major part of his own decisions; the Chamber of Commerce is guided by a full-time secretary, etc. Thus, decisions are made with the potentiality of the power structure in mind but few issues are clear in their implications for the powerful."

Rossi identifies three major sources of change in American communities: (1) professionals (public employees or executive directors of Chambers of Commerce and other civic groups); (2) competition among leaders and (3) the American value of progress. He notes that the function of citizen participation is to support, but not to create public policy; the function of the professional is to create.

Rossi notes that the type of community shapes the character of decision making. In communities where there is congruence between political structure and economic or social structures, decisions tend to be informally arrived at on a personal basis. In other more heterogeneous communities, political decision making is likely to bear little resemblance to decision making in other spheres. The greater the diversification of economic control, the less likely the concentration of power and the more likely healthy competition for leadership among different social positions in the community is likely to occur.

Rossi, Peter H. "Community Decision Making," *Administrative Science Quarterly* 1 (March 1957) 415-43.

The author reviews a number of studies dealing with community decisions and discusses the opportunities and problems associated with each approach. Three general types of studies are discussed: (1) those concerned with the characteristics of decision-makers and their relationship to the kinds of decisions made; (2) those which examine decision making seeking to understand the processes by which persons make choices; and (3) those focusing on the partisans of issues. The last of these is probably of greatest interest to students of community power. It involves three basic research designs: (1) studies which focus on those who are in a position to influence decisions or decision makers; (2) studies of power or influence reputations; and (3) studies of particular issues in which influence or power have played a part in the determination of the outcome.

Rossi suggests a number of questions for further research. He notes that while it is impossible to make clear statements about the variations in decision making which one might expect in diverse types of communities, the following community characteristics seem to be related to patterns of influence: (1) economic diversity; (2) political homogeneity; (3) degree of social and economic autonomy; and (4) community growth.

Rossi, Peter H. "Community Decision Making," in Roland Young, ed., *Approaches to the Study of Politics* (Evanston, Ill.: Northwestern University Press, 1958) pp. 363-82.

Salisbury, Robert H. "Urban Politics: The New Convergence of Power," *Journal of Politics* 26 (November 1964) 775-97.

Salisbury examines the literature on urban history and community power and attempts to develop some generalizations about the structure of political power in relatively large cities. He stresses the importance of the changing character and scope of the matters with which government has dealt in urban areas. He concludes that this changing subject matter, among other things, has led to a "new convergence of power."

The power structure which characterizes many large cities, and to which other cities are evolving, is typically comprised of a coalition of locally-oriented economic interests headed by an elected chief of the city. However, the professional public servant (i.e., the planner, engineer, manager and school superintendent) is the major innovative force in the power structure. "The bulk of the city's working agenda is made up of proposals drawn up by the city's own technicians to meet problems identified by them or their allies in the problem-oriented sectors of the community." For Salisbury, the problem-oriented sectors of the community are downtown business groups whose interest is not so much in perquisites but in community stability and in maintaining or attaining a high level of community services.

Sayre, Wallace S., and Polsby, Nelson W. "American Political Science and Urbanization," in Leo Schnore and Phillip Hauser, eds., *The Study of Urbanization* (New York: John Wiley and Sons, Inc., 1965) pp. 115-56.

The authors review the past accomplishments of social scientists, especially political scientists, in the study of urban politics and make a number of fairly specific suggestions as to the necessary directions of future research. In discussing the question of community power, the authors review the literature and conclude that the view that American communities are dominated by a generally powerful, cohesive, economic elite has been discredited. This "elitist" view, they say, was based on insufficient evidence and gathered by misleading and inadequate research techniques.

Sayre and Polsby suggest that little further progress toward a theory of community power will be made without turning to comparative studies. They note that the simple classification of communities as either elite-dominated or pluralistic is inadequate for analytical purposes. When undertaking comparative studies, it will be necessary to specify various types of political systems and to inspect the social, demographic, economic, legal, institutional and cultural patterns which seem to be related to each type of distribution of power.

Sjoberg, Gideon. "Urban Community Theory and Research: A Partial Evaluation," *American Journal of Economics and Sociology* 14 (January 1955) 199-206.

The author argues that a major oversight of most persons who have studied American communities is that they have neglected to study the impact of factors external to the community on the nature of life in that community. For example, decisions made by surrounding communities and by higher levels of government have an impact on both the physical ecology of the community and the autonomy and authority of its social, political and economic institutions. Thus, local decisions may not be a function only of the distribution of influence and the availability of resources within the community, but may be strongly shaped by decisions made outside the community itself.

Spinrad, William. "Power in Local Communities," *Social Problems* 12 (Winter 1965) 335-56.

The author surveys the literature on community power and discusses the advantages and disadvantages of various research techniques. He also examines the findings on the distribution of influence and seeks to account for the reasons why certain groups or types of individuals tend to be involved in decision making in certain kinds of communities under certain situations under certain circumstances, but not in others. He concludes that most American cities are relatively pluralistic. Power is widely dispersed on some questions but not on others. On the most salient questions, even though many groups may affect what is ultimately decided upon, the determinative leadership comes from some combination of particular interest groups, local government officials, professionals and experts.

Spinrad states that the primary types of power resources are: (1) formal position; (2) access to formal decision-makers; (3) values which are congruent with those of the community as a whole (which provide legitimacy for non-governmental officials much in the same way that formal position provides legitimacy for government officials); (4) money; and (5) the size of the interest constituency of which one is a part. He notes an important limit on the use of power in communities which has not received adequate attention from students of community power is the relationship between the power structure and superior governments. These links may be weak or strong; the stronger the link the more resources the community has to effectuate its will.

Straits, Bruce C. "Community Adoption and Implementation of Urban Renewal," *American Journal of Sociology* 71 (July 1965) 77-82.

This article is a critical analysis of an article by Amos Hawley entitled "Community Power and Urban Renewal Success" which appeared in the *American Journal of Sociology* 68 (June 1963) 422-31. The author argues that the proportion of managers, proprietors and officials in the total labor force is not an adequate measure of the concentration of power in communities and concludes that a city's size and the age of its housing are better predictors of urban renewal success.

Swanson, Bert E. "Community Leadership and Policy Implementation," *Community Leadership and Decision Making* (Iowa City, Iowa: Institute of Public Affairs, University of Iowa, 1966) pp. 48-57.

The author draws distinctions between open and closed community political systems on the basis of findings developed by himself, Robert Agger and Daniel Goldrich in their study of four communities in different parts of the country. He discusses the implications of these different systems for the implementation of public policy, especially policies which involve federal programs. He briefly suggests some ways that those interested in community action might best use their resources in the context of each type of political system.

Sw.anson, Bert E., ed. *Current Trends in Comparative Community Studies* (Kansas City: Community Studies, Inc., 1962).

This volume is a report on a 1961 conference on community policy making held in Kansas City. The proceedings of the conference are summarized and the papers presented are reproduced. The authors of the papers are M. Kent Jennings, David Rogers, Marshall N. Goldstein, Bradbury Seasholes, Robert C. Stone, and Robert Agger, Bert E. Swanson and Daniel Goldrich. (A review of each of these articles can be found in this bibliography under the author's name.)

Walton, John. "Substance and Artifact: The Current Status of Research and Community Power Structure," *American Journal of Sociology* 71 (January 1966) 430-38.

The author classifies thirty-three separate studies dealing with fifty-five different communities according to various characteristics of those communities, the methods used by the researchers and the findings. He concludes that findings that rely on a single method might well be an artifact of that method; i.e., the reputational method tends to identify pyramidal power structure while the decision-making approach discovers factional and coalitional power structures. This tendency is more pronounced when the two-step reputational method is used as compared to a direct nomination procedure.

Walton also finds that (1) socially integrated heterogeneous populations, and those in the northeast and north central regions of the country as compared to those in the south, have less concentrated power structures; and (2) economic variables reflecting patterns characteristic of increasing industrialization are moderately associated with less concentrated power structures.

Walton, John. "Vertical Axis and Community Power," *Southwestern Social Science Quarterly* 48 (December 1967) 353-68.

The author examines what he describes as "the existing body of community power structure studies," and finds that these studies show that competitive power structures are associated with: absentee ownership, adequate economic resources, satellite status, and political party competition. A number of other variables are investigated and found to be statistically unrelated to the nature of the power structure. Walton interprets his finding in the context of Roland Warren's theory of the vertical axis of community organization. He holds that each of the variables he found to be related to competitive power structure is related to greater intercommunity dependence and he argues that interdependence tends to produce a fragmentation of the local normative order, as well as the introduction of new resources and sanctions, which lead to a more competitive power arrangement. On the basis of his findings he suggests some directions of future research.

This article originally appeared in Terry Clark, ed., *Community Structure and Decision-Making: Comparative Analyses* (San Francisco: Chandler Publishing Co., 1968) pp. 441-59.

Warren, Roland L. "Toward a Typology of Extra-Community Controls Limiting Local Community Autonomy," *Social Forces* 34 (May 1956) 338-41.

The author studies policy making in an unincorporated area in New York called "Dairyville" (population 1,351) to determine those factors which restrict the local community's capacity to determine the social, political and economic policies which decide the quality of life in the community. Factors by which one might identify the relative autonomy of communities are identified and discussed. It is noted the controls in the local community are both formal and informal, the latter involving such factors as cultural patterns, informal group structure, feelings of local autonomy, and economic competition outside the community.

Westby, David L. "The Civic Sphere in the American City," *Social Forces* 45 (December 1966) 161-70.

The author argues that the elites of public life in American cities, unlike European cities, are structurally bifurcated into civic and political spheres. Urban politics has low status; urban civic spheres have high status. He examines the reasons why this bifurcation has taken place. He "assumes" that economic elites actually dominate the community policy making although they are not, in his view, necessarily cohesive. He argues that accountability in the civic spheres is diffuse, which thus allows more freedom of action (or nonaction) than leaders in the government sphere enjoy. The bifurcation enhances the power of economic dominants by freeing them from restraints inherent upon government, by allowing them to maximize their prestige source and providing them access to public affairs with considerable legitimacy.

Whitten, Norman E., Jr. "Power Structure and Sociocultural Change in Latin American Communities," *Social Forces* 43 (March 1965) 320-29.

Based on the findings of nineteen community studies in eight Latin American countries, the author concludes that movement from folk to national cultural orientation of the community level is the function of increasing size and urbanization. An expanding population and concomitant changes in the socioeconomic character of the community is a general pattern in Latin America which results in a decrease in the structure of community powers dependent upon local religious-magic institutions and less parochial in character. These changes lead to a development of a community power structure more closely tied to the economic structure in the community and one which is increasingly similar to that at the national level in its general characteristics.

Williams, Oliver P. "A Typology for Comparative Local Government," *Midwest Journal of Political Science* 5 (May 1961) 150-64.

The author suggests that an analysis of local politics can be facilitated by examining the images which government officials have of the substantitive and instrumental roles of the local government. On the basis of his study of four middle-sized cities, the author develops a four-cell typology of local governments. These cells correspond to the following four images of the role of government: (1) it is the instrument of community growth; (2) it is the provider of amenities; (3) its primary functions should be limited to "caretaker" functions and; (4) government is an arbiter of conflicting interests. He discusses some of the various consequences of these different community ethos.

Wingfield, Clyde J. "Power Structure and Decision Making in City Planning," *Public Administration Review* 23 (1963) 74-80.

This article briefly summarizes the relevance of some of the studies of community power to the role of the city planner. He suggests that the planner's skill and knowledge give him an advantage in the pecking order of the community power structure. "Like wealth or social status, professional skill and knowledge may be translated into power." Wingfield points out that the potential for power is not equivalent to its exercise. He suggests some ways in which planners might make the best use of their power resources to improve the quality of life in the community.

Wrong, Dennis Hume. "Who Runs American Cities," *New Society* 1 (April 1963) 16-17.

The author evaluates the results of recent community power studies and notes that three main patterns of community power have been revealed: (1) the ruling elite model in which community decision making is monopolized by local economic dominants; (2) the power vacuum type in which economic dominants have withdrawn from local decision making, leaving no group with a clear responsibility for local decisions; and (3) "pluralistic" patterns in which local politicians lead coalitions of all groups in the community and provide forceful leadership. The author states that students of community power have largely ignored larger metropolitan centers and suggests that while "pluralism" will be the characteristic pattern of influence in these communities it is likely to be anarchistic in character, rather than a more politically creative type of pluralism which Robert Dahl found in his study of New Haven, Connecticut.

Yager, John W. "Who Runs Our Town," *National Civic Review* 52 (May 1963) 255-59.

The author discusses various aspects of formal political leadership in local communities and stresses the decline of partisan political influence and the causes and consequences of that phenomenon. He argues that the literature on community power or community studies suggests four potential sources of political leadership in the community: (1) from economic institutions; (2) the mass media; (3) minority groups; and (4) independent political citizen action groups. The author's conclusions appear to be based on a rather uncritical examination of some of the community power studies, as well as his own intuitive analysis of political leadership at the local level.

DISSERTATIONS

Agger, Robert E. "The Dynamics of Local Political Participation: Empirical Research and Theoretical Inquiry," Ph.D., University of Oregon, 1954.

Allegrucci, Robert L. "An Analysis of the Social Structure and Ideological Sources of Elitism: A Comparative Study of Community Power," Ph.D., University of Missouri, Columbia, 1969. (Order No. 70-2953) m $3.95; x $13.95. 307 pp.

Andrews, W.H. "Some Correlates of Rural Leadership and Social Power among Inter-community Leaders," Ph.D., Michigan State University, 1956.

Blumberg, Leonard. "Community Leaders: The Social Bases and Social Psychological Concomitants of Community Power," Ph.D., University of Michigan, 1955.

Bonjean, Charles Michael. "Community Leadership: A Conceptual Refinement and Comparative Analysis," Ph.D., The University of North Carolina at Chapel Hill, 1963. (Order No. 64-9406) m $3.00; x $9.70.

Buck, Robert E. "Power, Ideology, and Decision Making: An Investigation in the Social Psychology of Community Politics," Ph.D., University of Texas at Austin, 1970. (Order No. 71-102) 175 pp.

Clelland, Donald A. "Occupational Composition and Community Structure: A Study of the Impact of Professionalization on Community Life and Stratification Patterns," Ph.D., Michigan State University, 1970. (Order No. 70-20, 445) m $4.00; x $10.15. 222 pp.

Danzger, Murray Herbert. "Civil Rights Conflict and Community Power Structure," Ph.D., Columbia University, 1968. (Order No. 69-15, 667) m $3.40; x $11.95.

Galbo, Charles Joseph. "Personality and Influence in a Community Power Structure," Ph.D., University of Arizona, 1962. (Order No. 63-2581) m $3.00; x $4.80.

Grimes, Michael D. "Some Structural Correlates of Leadership Arrangements: A Study of Seventeen Communities," Ph.D., University of Texas at Austin, 1970. (Order No. 71-11, 547) 148 pp.

Griswold, L. "The Community as a Social System: A Study in Comparative Analysis," Ph.D., University of Kentucky, 1956.

Jennings, Myron Kent. "Political Statuses and Political Roles in Community Decision Making," Ph.D., University of North Carolina, 1961. (Order No. 63-3539) m $4.30; x $15.10.

Johnson, Kenneth. "Urbanization and Political Change in Latin America," Ph.D., University of California, Los Angeles, 1963.

Johnson, Rogers Pyke. "Community Democracy and Power: A Study of Conflicting Themes in the Sociological Conception of Community Power," Ph.D., Brandeis University, 1968. (Order No. 68-12, 436) m $6.35; x $22.50.

Johnstone, Ronald Lavern. "Militant and Conservative Community Leadership among Negro Clergymen," Ph.D., University of Michigan, 1963. (Order No. 64-8178) m $3.00; x $9.25.

McFatter, William T., Jr. "The Degree, Level, Pattern, and Efficacy of Citizen Participation in Policy Matters under Different Types of Community Power Structure," Ed.D., University of Florida, 1970. (Order No. 71-12, 765) 128 pp.

McKee, James B. "Organized Labor and Community Decision Making," Ph.D., University of Wisconsin, 1953.

Mauger, Karl Frederick. "The Use of Public Relations and Human Power Structure to Promote the Educational Program within a Community," Ed.D., Pennsylvania State University, 1965. (Order No. 66-8741) m $3.00; x $5.80.

Miller, Kenneth Edward. "The Structural Correlates of Community Power Systems," Ph.D., Duke University, 1965. (Order No. 65-8813) m $3.00; x $7.40.

Miller, Paul A. "A Comparative Analysis of the Decision Process: Community Organization toward Major Health Goals," Ph.D., Michigan State University, 1954.

Mulford, Charles Lee. "Some Relationships between Formal Organizations, Community Problems and Leadership," Ph.D., Iowa State University of Science and Technology, 1962. (Order No. 62-3023) m $3.00; x $8.60.

Teague, Richard L. "Community Power and Social Change: A Case for Social Action," Ph.D., North Carolina State University at Raleigh, 1969. (Order No. 70-9228) m $3.00; x $8.00. 175 pp.

Thorp, Robert Kent. "The Role of the Daily Newspaper Publisher in the Community Power Structure," Ph.D., State University of Iowa, 1963. (Order No. 64-3434) m $6.45; x $22.75.

Reichler, Melvin Litwack. "Community Power Structure in Action," Ph.D., University of Michigan, 1963. (Order No. 63-5008) m $3.15; x $11.05.

Wenger, Dennis E. "Toward a Comparative Model for the Analysis of Community Power: A Conceptualization and Empirical Application," Ph.D., Ohio State University, 1970. (Order No. 71-7593) 437 pp.

Chapter 5

DEFINING AND MEASURING SOCIAL POWER

Some of the most difficult problems in the study of community power involve the conceptualization and measurement of power and influence. Serious students of community power will want to spend some time with the general literature on the study of power. However, the amount of literature available is vast. In this brief chapter a number of those pieces which seem to offer perspectives which are more helpful than others in the analysis of community power are cited without annotation. If asked to recommend items which seem the most significant for the development of a theory of community power, we would suggest those identified by an asterisk preceding the authors' names.

Abramson, E.; Cutter, H.A.; Kautz, R.W.; and Mendelson, M. "Social Power and Commitment: A Theoretical Statement," *American Sociological Review* 23 (February 1958) 15-22.

Adams, J.S., and Romney, A.K. "A Functional Analysis of Authority," *Psychological Review* 66 (1959) 234-51.

Barber, James David. *Power in Committees: An Experiment in the Governmental Process* (Chicago: Rand McNally, 1966).

Bennis, W.G.; Berkowitz, N.; Affinito, M.; and Malone, M. "Authority, Power and the Ability to Influence," *Human Relations* 11, No. 2 (1958) 143-55.

Bensman, Joseph, and Vidich, Arthur. "Power Cliques in Bureaucratic Society," *Social Research* 29 (Winter 1962) 467-74.

Bierstadt, Robert. "An Analysis of Social Power," *American Sociological Review* 15 (December 1950) 730-38.

*Blau, Peter M. *Exchange and Power in Social Life* (New York: John Wiley, 1964).

Blumer, Herbert. "Social Structure and Power Conflict," in A. Kornhauser, ed., *Industrial Conflict* (New York: McGraw Hill, 1954) pp. 232-39.

Brams, Steven J. "Measuring the Concentration of Power in Political Systems," *American Political Science Review* 62 (June 1968) 461-75.

*Cartwright, Dorwin. "Influence, Leadership, Control," in James March, ed., *Handbook of Organizations* (Chicago: Rand McNally, 1965) pp. 1-43.

Cartwright, Dorwin. *Studies in Social Power* (Ann Arbor: Center for Social Research, University of Michigan, 1959).

Dahl, Robert A. "Cause and Effect in the Study of Politics," in Daniel Lerner, ed., *Cause and Effect* (New York: The Free Press, 1965) pp. 75-98.

Dahl, Robert A. *Modern Political Analysis,* 2d. ed. (Englewood Cliffs, N.J.: Prentice-Hall, Inc., 1970).

*Dahl, Robert A. "Power" in *International Encyclopedia of the Social Sciences* (New York: Macmillan and Free Press, 1968), vol. 12, pp. 405-15.

Dahl, Robert A. "The Concept of Power,"*Behavioral Science* 2 (July 1957) 201-15.

Davison, W.P. *Power – The Idea and Its Communication,* P-1869. (Santa Monica, Calif.: The RAND Corporation, 1959).

Deutsch, Karl. *Nerves of Government* (New York: The Free Press, 1963).

*Deutsch, Karl. "On the Concepts of Politics and Power," *Journal of International Affairs* 21 (2) (1967) 232-41.

Emerson, Richard M. "Power-Dependence Relations," *American Sociological Review* 27 (February 1962) 31-41.

French, J.R.P., Jr. "A Formal Theory of Social Power," *Psychological Review* 63 (May 1956) 181-94.

French, J.R.P., Jr., and Snyder, R. "Leadership and Interpersonal Power," in Dorwin Cartwright, ed., *Studies in Social Power* (Ann Arbor: University of Michigan, Institute for Social Research, 1959) pp. 118-49.

*French, J.R.P., Jr., and Raven, Bertram. "The Bases of Social Power," in Dorwin Cartwright, ed., *Studies in Social Power* (Ann Arbor: University of Michigan, Institute for Social Research, 1959) pp. 150-67.

Friedrich, Carl J. "Political Leadership and the Problem of Charismatic Power," *Journal of Politics* 23 (February 1961) 3-24.

*Gamson, William. *Power and Discontent* (Homewood, Ill.: Dorsey Press, 1969).

Gartly, E. Jaco. "Prestige and Esteem as Power Components: An Experimental Analysis," *Southwestern Social Science Quarterly* 33 (March 1953) 319-27.

Garvey, G. "The Domain of Politics," *Western Political Quarterly* 23 (March 1970) 120-37.

Gilman, G. "An Inquiry into the Nature and Use of Authority," in M. Haire, ed., *Organization Theory in Industrial Practice* (New York: Wiley, 1962), pp. 105-42.

Goffman, Irwin W. "Status Consistency and Preferences for Change in Power Distribution," *American Sociological Review* 22 (June 1957) 275-81.

Goldhamer, Herbert, and Shils, Edward A. "Types of Power and Status," *American Journal of Sociology* 45 (September 1939) 171-82.

Gouldner, A.W. "The Norm of Reciprocity: A Preliminary Statement," *American Sociological Review* 25 (April 1960) 161-78.

Harary, F., "A Criterion for Unanimity in French's Theory of Social Power," in Dorwin Cartwright, ed., *Studies in Social Power* (Ann Arbor: University of Michigan, Institute for Social Research, 1959) pp. 168-82.

Harris, E.E. "Political Power," *Ethics* 68 (October 1957) 1-10.

*Harsanyi, John. "Measurement of Social Power in N-Persons Reciprocal Power Situations," *Behavioral Science* 7 (January 1962) 81-91.

*Harsanyi, John. "Measurement of Social Power, Opportunity Costs and the Theory of Two-Person Bargaining Games," *Behavioral Science* 7 (January 1962) 67-80.

Homans, G.C. "Social Behavior as Exchange," *American Journal of Sociology* 63 (May 1958) 597-606.

Jessop, R.D. "Exchange and Power in Structural Analysis," *Sociological Review* 17 (November 1969) 415-31.

Janda, K.F. "Toward an Exploration of the Concept of Leadership in Terms of the Concept of Power," *Human Relations* 9, No. 13 (1960) 345-63.

Jouvenal, Bertrand de. *Power: The Natural History of Its Growth,* rev. ed. (London: Batchworth, 1952, first published in French in 1945).

Kaplan, Abraham. "Power in Perspective," in Robert Kahn and Elise Boulding, eds. *Power and Conflict in Organizations* (New York: Basic Books, 1964) pp. 11-32

Kimball, S.T., and Pearsall, M. "Event Analysis as an Approach to Community Study," *Social Forces* 34 (October 1955) 58-63.

Kornhauser, Arthur, ed. *Problems of Power in American Democracy* (Detroit: Wayne State University Press, 1957).

Lammers, C.J. "Power and Participation in Decision Making in Formal Organizations," *American Journal of Sociology* 73 (September 1967) 201-16.

Lasswell, Harold D. "Political Power and Democratic Values" in Arthur Kornhauser, ed., *Problems of Power in American Democracy* (Detroit: Wayne State University Press, 1957) pp. 57-91.

Lasswell, Harold D. *Power and Personality* (New York: Norton, 1948).

*Lasswell, Harold D., and Kaplan, Abraham. *Power and Society* (New Haven, Conn.: Yale University Press, 1950).

Lazarsfeld, Paul, and Katz, D. *Personal Influence* (Glencoe, Ill.: The Free Press, 1955).

Lenski, Gerhard. *Power and Privilege* (New York: McGraw-Hill, 1966).

Lippitt, R.; Polansky, N.; Redl, F.; and Rosen, S. "The Dynamics of Power," *Human Relations* 5, No. 1 (1952) 37-64.

Loewenstein, Karl. *Political Power and the Governmental Process* (Chicago: University of Chicago Press, 1957).

Lynd, Robert S. "Power in American Society as Resource and Problem," in Arthur Kornhauser, ed., *Problems of Power in American Democracy* (Detroit: Wayne State University Press, 1957) pp. 1-45.

*McFarland, Andrew S. *Power and Leadership in Pluralist Systems* (Stanford: Stanford University Press, 1969).

March, James G. "An Introduction to the Theory and Measurement of Influence," *American Political Science Review* 49 (June 1955) 431-51.

March, James G. "Influence Measurement in Experimental and Semi-Experimental Groups," *Sociometry* 19 (December 1956) 260-71.

March, James G. "Measurement Concepts in the Theory of Influence," *Journal of Politics* 19 (May 1957) 202-26.

*March, James G. "The Power of Power," in David Easton, ed., *Varieties of Political Theory* (Englewood Cliffs, N.J.: Prentice-Hall, 1966) pp. 39-70.

Merriam, Charles. *Political Power: Its Composition and Incidence* (New York: McGraw-Hill, 1934).

Michel, Jerry. "Measurement of Social Power on the Community Level," *American Journal of Economics and Sociology* 23 (April 1964) 189-96.

Morgenthau, Hans. "Power as a Political Concept," in Roland Young, ed., *Approaches to the Study of Politics* (Evanston: Northwestern University Press, 1958).

Nagel, Jack H. "Some Questions About the Concept of Power," *Behavioral Science* 13 (March 1968) 129-37.

Neely, Twila E. "The Sources of Political Power: A Contribution to the Sociology of Leadership," *American Journal of Sociology* 33 (March 1928) 769-83.

Neumann, Franz. "Approaches to the Study of Political Power," *Political Science Quarterly* 65 (June 1950) 161-80.

Padover, Saul K. "Lasswell's Impact on the Study of Power in Democracy," *Social Research* 29 (Winter 1962) 489-94.

Parsons, Talcott. "On the Concept of Influence," *Public Opinion Quarterly* 27 (Spring 1963), 37-62. A comment by J.S. Coleman appears on pp. 63-82; a communication by R.A. Bauer on pp. 83-86; and a rejoinder by Talcott Parsons on pp. 87-92.

*Parsons, Talcott. "On the Concept of Political Power," *Proceedings of the American Philosophical Society* 107 (June 1963) 232-62.

Parsons, Talcott. "Some Reflections on the Place of Force in Social Processes," in Harry Eckstein, ed., *Internal War* (New York: The Free Press, 1964) pp. 37-40.

Parsons, Talcott. "The Distribution of Power in American Society," *World Politics* 10 (1957) 123-43.

Parsons, Talcott. "The Political Aspect of Social Structure and Process," in David Easton, ed., *Varieites of Political Theory* (Englewood Cliffs, N.J.: Prentice-Hall, 1966) pp. 71-112.

Partridge, P.H. "Some Notes on the Concept of Power," *Political Studies* 11 (June 1963) 107-25.

Raths, Louis. "Power in Small Groups," *Journal of Educational Sociology* 28 (1954) 97-103.

Raven, B.H., and French, J.R.P., Jr. "Group Support, Legitimate Power and Social Influence," *Journal of Personality* 26 (September 1958) 400-408.

Raven, B.H., and French, J.R.P., Jr. "Legitimate Power, Coercive Power and Observability in Social Influence," *Sociometry* 21 (June 1958) 83-97.

Riker, William H. "A Test of the Adequacy of the Power Index," *Behavioral Science* 4 (April 1959) 120-31.

Riker, William H. "Some Ambiguities in the Notion of Power," *American Political Science Review* 58 (June 1964) 341-49.

Russell, Bertrand. *Power: A New Social Analysis* (London: Allen and Unwin, 1938).

Schermerhorn, Richard A. *Society and Power* (New York: Random House, 1961).

Shapley, L.S., and Shubik, M.A. "A Method for Evaluating the Distribution of Power in a Committee System," *American Political Science Review* 48 (September 1954) 787-92.

*Simon, Herbert. "Notes on the Observation and Measurement of Political Power," *Journal of Politics* 15 (November 1953) 500-516.

Snyder, Richard C.; Bruck, H.W.; and Sapin, Burton. "The Decision-Making Approach" in H. Eulau, S.J. Eldersveld, and M. Janowitz, eds., *Political Behavior* (New York: The Free Press, 1956) pp. 352-58.

Tannenbaum, Arnold. "An Event Structure Approach to Social Power and to the Problem of Power Comparability," *Behavioral Science* 7 (July 1962) 315-31.

Walter, Benjamin. "On the Logical Analysis of Power Attribution Procedures," *Journal of Politics* 26 (November 1964) 850-66.

Walter, E.V. "Power and Violence," *American Political Science Review* 58 (June 1964) 350-60.

*Weber, Max. *The Theory of Social and Economic Organization,* edited by Talcott Parsons (Glencoe, Ill.: Free Press, 1957). First published as Part 1 of *Wirtschaft und Gesellschaft* (1922).

Wrong, Dennis H. "Some Problems in Defining Social Power," *American Journal of Sociology* 73 (May 1968) 673-81.

AUTHOR INDEX